..... author and business consultant, Joan Baker is committed to helping others get the life they want. Joan is a company director and consultant to a broad range of large businesses and SMEs in private and not-for-profit organisations both in Ireland and abroad. She has written eight books specialising in helping individuals and organisations achieve success. Currently residing in New Zealand, Joan works internationally as a skilled consultant in high performance. She can be contacted at jbaker@gallarus.co.nz.

Joanne Hession is a successful entrepreneur and recognised leader in training, mentoring and business in Ireland. Joanne is responsible for training thousands of budding entrepreneurs through her business QED Training (www.QED training.ie) and works internationally in the Business School sector through QED International (www.QEDinternational.ie). She is passionate about business and providing new businesses with best in class training on how to do business better, smarter and more successfully. She can be contacted at Joanne@qedtraining.ie.

MERCIER PRESS

Cork

www.mercierpress.ie

ISBN: 978 1 78117 138 7

10 9 8 7 6 5 4 3 2 1

A CIP record for this title is available from the British Library

Printed and bound in the EU.

CONTENTS

A Note from the Authors

As we finalise this book in December 2012, we are only too aware that we are living in a time of difficult economic conditions and that these conditions may continue for quite a while. It may not seem, therefore, like the most opportune time to consider setting up a business, but we strongly believe that in these conditions owning your own business may be a much better use of your talents and energies than scrambling to obtain employment. Be aware, however, that there is much more to owning a business than simply becoming self-employed! Business creation is not just about one job for one person, it's about building a wealth-creating asset that delivers value and employment for the owner and for others.

The majority of entities described as businesses are no such thing! Many trades-people, professionals, contractors and consultants merely have a job rather than owning and running a business. It's relatively easy to register an occupation as a business and begin to work. Unfortunately, that is all many who consider themselves business owners do. A technician rather than an entrepreneur sets up most such businesses, immediately getting busy doing the technical work that they are good at and neglecting to work on and develop an actual business.

When, therefore, you start in business for yourself it pays to think about it as a business concern (i.e. a separate entity from yourself) right from the start. Whether you envisage it as always remaining small or eventually becoming large, the same basic principles apply.

We have spent a collective fifty years working in and on businesses, managing others, observing what works and what doesn't. We are both driven to achieve success and we both have a passion for helping others succeed. We decided to write this book in order to share many of the useful things we have observed, lessons we have learned and positive business techniques we have experienced and taught with success.

Whether you are already in business, or still thinking about setting up, we hope you will find the ideas in this book constructive and helpful. We suggest that you read it with a pen and paper to hand, so that you can note what you need to do for your enterprise to give it the best chance of flourishing.

How to use this book

Business books can be confusing and overwhelming as there are so many subjects and issues to discuss. We have tried to keep this book as simple as possible by organising it into only three sections:

1. The first section looks at you as a business owner, and the special mindset you need to have to run your business successfully.

2. The second section considers the organisation of your business and how you can step back from its day-to-day running to free up time to enable you to think strategically and make longer term plans for its development and for your personal life.

3. The third section looks at the people you work with: your employees and your customers. It tells you what you need to know to attract and retain great staff and loyal customers for the long-term, successful growth of your business.

Hopefully, this will allow you to dip into whichever subject has the most use or more immediate relevance for you.

We think that good questions can often be even more useful than answers, so we have sprinkled 'Killer Questions' throughout the book. The idea is for you to learn to ask the important questions whenever appropriate – then, even as your business and circumstances change, you will focus on the essential matters. Again, it's a good idea to write these questions down, answer them and work out what changes you need to make to help your business thrive. Answers vary from business to business and from time to time, but good questions rarely change!

We hope this book helps you achieve the success you are looking for with your business. We'd love to hear about your experiences and your suggestions as to how you feel we could help further. You can contact us through our website, www.dontgetajobbuildabusiness.com.

Joan & Joanne

INTRODUCTION: OWNING A BUSINESS v. OWNING A JOB

There are several things that distinguish those whose goal is to run a successful business (business owners) and those whose goal is simply to create a job for themselves and never to develop a business (the self-employed). The real difference is in the mindset. Business owners have a different attitude. Here are some of the most important things that they think and do:

A business owner uses income to develop capital

To the self-employed, income is the whole point, as they need it to live. To the business owner, profit (and positive cash flow) is a resource for reinvesting in the business and growing the concern. After all costs (including the owner's wage) have been covered, the surplus is used for developing new products and services to make the business more valuable. The whole point is to generate wealth through satisfying the needs of customers or clients. It is not that income doesn't matter to a business, of course it does, it's what is done with it that's different.

A business owner works on the business rather than in it

The self-employed are likely to be busy working every hour to deliver products or services. The business owner, by contrast, is focused on building an enterprise that can run without the owner – a business with other staff, a place with structure, systems and processes, a concern with clients and customers who don't relate only to the owner. In short the business owner is building something which is independent and ultimately saleable. The business runs the self-employed person, while the business owner runs the business.

A business owner has a plan for the business

In difficult financial times like these, many are driven to set up in business because jobs are scarce and it seems like the best or only option. Of these, the self-employed are seeking income and security, while the true business owner has a plan for what the business (however small at inception) could become. They are already thinking about the eventual nature of their business, how it could grow, who might ultimately buy it (or manage it) and how it would be distinctive.

A business owner develops goodwill

The self-employed are usually much too busy doing their work to focus on where they are headed. The business owner, on the other hand, knows that ultimately a great deal of the wealth they generate will come from goodwill: the intangibles that belong to the business. The kinds of things that make up goodwill include:

- brand awareness and reputation
- good management practices
- competent and loyal staff
- great customer lists
- good supplier relationships.

A business owner is seeking appropriate returns

The primary focus for many self-employed people is selling their time and skills. Business owners, by contrast, are very clear that they are looking for an appropriate return on both their time and their capital. Business owners take considerable risks. In addition they are well aware of the security of paid employment and all of the benefits that usually come with this – sick leave pay, redundancy provisions, health insurance, etc. They are also aware of the opportunity cost – what could be done with the time and money that is invested in their business? So business owners are looking for much more than a wage: they are seeking a return on their investment commensurate with the capital, skill and time they have invested in it.

A business owner wears a strategic hat

The self-employed person thinks like an employee and often regards administration, management and finding new customers as interruptions to the work they have to do, e.g. complaining that they only managed to clock up three hours of billable time in a day because of time spent training the apprentice, dealing with customer complaints or filing the VAT return! Business owners, on the other hand, are thinking about the leadership and management of the business and the development of capital. One is tactical in outlook: 'Where is my work coming from today and what will I get from it?' The other, the business owner, is strategic and thinking longer term about what the business needs to do to thrive. These roles are often incompatible. It's not that business owners don't need to do any real work in the business. Of course they do, but their focus and mindset is different from that of the self-employed.

SECTION 1:
YOURSELF

Let's start with you! Let us suppose that you have already or wish to set yourself up in business – either as a sole trader or a company – and are wondering how are you going to make a go of it, keep it growing and really create value from it. A true business, as opposed to self-employment, needs to develop and grow. Be assured that your business is never going to be better than you are. There are some important and difficult questions, therefore, which you need to ask yourself before you take this life-changing step. For example, how good do you personally need to be to allow your business to succeed? What improvements do you need to make? How will you keep changing and developing personally at a rate that will allow your business to grow and thrive?

For all the usual esteem and adulation of high profile CEOs, bigger businesses are far less dependent on individuals than are smaller concerns. In large corporations there is almost always an executive team of highly qualified and experienced people involved. Small businesses, on the other hand, rarely have such an inherent comparative advantage. They are usually composed of very few people, often just you, the owner, to begin with, and so are much more exposed to the consequences of your behaviour.

So what sorts of things do you need to focus on? It's all too easy to put all the focus on the operational side of the business: the product/service, the customers, the staff you need, your premises, etc. It's tempting to dive in and work really hard on these issues and forget that you need to be in the right space and thinking straight from the start. Your business will only be as good as you are and will never change unless you do – make no changes and the future is staring you in the face. Your business will never grow unless you do – what aspects of yourself, therefore, need to be developed? In this section we go through the issues you need to consider before you go any further with your business and we give you some pointers on how to address them.

What's the Dream?

A considerable amount of nonsense has been spoken and written about business vision over the years and you may have been one of those cynical employees who has had to sit through corporate presentations on management's vision of the concern's mission and to pay homage to the 'mission statement' plaques in the corporate reception area. But like many fashions and fads there is a germ of real insight at the core of the concept of the mission statement – in other words the dream for the corporation. Everyone involved in a business enterprise should be aware of and buy into the mission of the business that employs them and what, therefore, they collectively aspire to attain.

It is very important that you should have a dream for your own life. What do you really want? What would be an ideal life for you? What do you need in order to attain that life? Much of this will come down to developing the wealth that will allow you the freedom to live the life you want. We have more to say later about achieving financial freedom through your business (see page 44).

As a business owner, you will be relying on your business to help you achieve the life of your dreams. You may hope to build a business that you can sell for a substantial sum, or your ideal may be a successful business with great cash flow which allows you a rewarding lifestyle that includes continuing to manage or govern your business. Indeed, working hard in your business may itself be a part of your dream existence. Whether or not you wish to retire rich or continue to run a business for decades, the success of your business will usually be essential to attaining your dream.

You need a dream for your business, too, in order to make it as successful as possible. This is not about wordsmith-ing clever slogans or coming up with wishful thinking PowerPoint presentations. Rather, having a realistic dream or vision for your business is about having a view about what you are trying to create. Your dream may be a picture you can see clearly in your head or a story you can tell about the destination you want to reach. The whole point of clarifying the dream for your business is that it provides a guide: for you about what you are creating and for others who will work with you towards that end. If you already have others working with you it is a good idea to get them involved in discussing or refining the business vision.

Clear dreams are compelling – they make us want to do the things we need to do to make them come true. They demand a stretch: if they were easy we would have achieved them long ago. Compelling dreams provide meaning. *If I am to devote years of my life to this I need to see a reason why it is worthwhile. Nobody gets out of bed for a number!* It's tempting to try to run your business through financials or key ratios or performance indicators of some sort. These are all useful of course, but they are not at all inspiring. People always want to know why they should sign up, why they should make an extra effort. This is why being able to talk about the wonderful things your business will do, if you can get it right, matters so much. Well-described visions make it obvious what you need to do, they highlight priorities and make it easier for you to choose what to do next. It becomes easier to set goals and to measure your progress, because you know what you are trying to achieve and how to monitor whether you are achieving it. The more people you have around, the more important it is that everyone is on the same page: everyone is clear about what you are trying to achieve – the dream, the vision for your business – and everyone knows the path you need to follow to attain that dream.

What do you value?

We all have values. So do organisations. We may have spent very little time working out our own values or those that drive our business, but others can usually see clearly what it is we care about as a person or what factors a business values. It's worth the effort to be clear about what matters to you so you can make sure you can honour that in your whole life. Your business is unlikely to make you happy unless it is a good fit with your personal values. Likewise your business is unlikely to thrive unless you are clear about exactly what your business values. It's all too easy to think you have to value everything: customer service, innovation, speed, creativity, diversity, personal touch, etc. However, while all of these are undoubtedly 'good' things, it is impossible to make more than a few things a hallmark of your organisation. So what does your business really need to value? And how would your customers know that you value these things? Another way to look at this question is to ask: what drives you?

You need to have a clear answer to these questions in your head, which is best achieved by putting it down on paper before you proceed. *Life's too short to live someone else's dream!*

What's Your Role?

Killer Question

What's the stuff that only I can do?

Despite all the hype about celebrity CEOs, small and medium-sized enterprises are far more reliant on their owner/manager than any big corporation is on its chief executive who, more often than not, is surrounded by an executive team of highly qualified and experienced people. That makes your role as owner/manager and how you conduct yourself far more critical to your business. The business is a reflection of you.

Many businesses start with only the business owner and an idea. The problem with this model is that the owner may become used to doing everything. This is a very limiting concept and hugely constrains the business potential. Your business can never get any bigger when you follow this type of model! Even if you start alone you need to do so with a view to developing and expanding the business and having a mindset already focused on this objective.

Don't get a job!

If you want to be successful in business you should not see yourself as self-employed, owning a 'job'; you are a business owner. Beware of giving yourself a job – working long hours, at high risk, for relatively poor pay! Yes, you will have to work hard, but your role is also to work *on* the business rather than just *in* it. Too many business owners get completely waylaid working all the hours possible in their business. They have simply created a job for them-selves – and usually a poor one. The real problem with that is that no-one is working *on* the business – running it well, seeking out growth opportunities, developing the products, services and people that will make it great. A good way to make sure that you don't get mired in working *in* the business is to set aside a morning a week (or one day a month, or whatever) to focus on bigger issues, such as strategy, growth, brand or planning. This is best done away from your usual place of work as it is too easy otherwise to slip back to doing what you normally do.

Working on the business – what must you do?

There are aspects of your business that must be handled by the owner/manager with or without professional assistance – developing strategy and direction, perhaps meeting with key clients or suppliers, dealing with the bank or venture capitalists, handling public relations, recruitment, etc. It is important you are clear about the things that are essential for your role to undertake so that you ensure you are spending most of your time on the functions which allow you personally to control your business or that you are good at. The rest needs to be outsourced or delegated to staff.

What are you good at?

It's important to be clear about what it is that you bring to your business. Most of us are only good at a small number of things. Consider where your strengths lie – marketing, networking, selling, financing, organisation, innovation, leadership, people – and resolve to focus as much as you can in that area. It's the things we don't do well that are often critical to identify – where will you need help and where will you get it?

The business won't outperform you!

Small businesses tend to be a reflection of the person who set them up. That means your attitude and your behaviour are critical to the success of your enterprise. What kinds of attitudes do you bring to your business? How do you behave in your business and what are your standards like? All of this will be obvious to both customers and staff. Successful business owners tend to be positive, optimistic, can-do kinds of people. They are good at attracting others who want to do business with them and work in their business. They hold themselves to very high standards of behaviour – ethical, fair, good to be around. Staff will look to you to set an example – they will never treat customers and suppliers any better than you treat them. Where do you need to set the bar so that your business can become great? Ask yourself if any of your habits or attitudes need a tune up – don't allow yourself to hold your business back.

What kind of culture will you create?

Culture is simply 'the way we do things around here' or as we heard a client say recently, 'what you do when no one is watching!' So culture is simply the set of behaviours that your employees think are normal or acceptable in your business. That will include things like the way they treat each other and people outside the organisation. It will include the kind of communication they think is appropriate between themselves and with your customers. In short, when this is good it is very, very good (and very valuable to your business) and when it is bad it is horrid! When there is a good culture people do the right thing and they do it as well as they can even without supervision. With a poor or inappropriate culture, your business is on its way down each day.

You won't be able to achieve the culture you want overnight, but you will need to be clear about what you want and vigilant about bringing it about. Think about yourself as a role model. Be careful about what you reward and reinforce. Consider well what you will draw attention to and correct. Look for the behaviours you want and seek to get more of them; stamp out the ones that will damage your reputation, both inside and out. At any one time there will be habits and behaviours that you want more of and those you want to see less: be clear what's on each list and work hard to get what you want. Remember, they are all watching you.

Personal Productivity

What's the point of having a great dream and wonderful ideas if you can't get anything done? We all get derailed at times – too many meetings, email, doing too much ourselves, competing demands from our other roles in life. In the end, the prizes go to effective people – those who can identify the priorities and make sure that most of their time is spent in areas that give a really good return on their efforts and skills. That's so easy to say and ever so hard to do on a consistent basis.

Killer Questions

What are the most important things that need to be done?
What can I get other people to do for me?

In this chapter we detail some of the best methods to become more effective.

Audit your behaviour

The word 'audit' sends shivers down the spine, but nothing beats good data. Keep a log for a few weeks and account for your time – using five to six minute intervals like lawyers or accountants is a great way to do this (how do you think they focus in order to rack up all those billable hours?). Of course, you don't have to stop to record what you're doing every few minutes, but at the end of each thirty- or sixty- or ninety-minute period jot down or use an app to record what you have spent your time doing. We still do this from time to time. It will provide you with a great reality check and stop you getting complacent. And watch what you do outside work – there's no point in toiling frantically for a few hours at work and then frittering the rest of your time away – audit the full twenty-four hours. You'll be amazed at where your time goes and how little value you get.

Limit the 'to do' list

Many of us use these like a wish list – and there isn't a chance of everything on it happening in a day! Further-more, it looks overwhelming. We also mix up the essential with the trivial. By all means have a 'catch all' list – some-where to dump every passing 'must do sometime' thought. But to get your 'to do' list working well for you is really simple: identify the most important two to three things you must do today and work on number one until it is finished. This sounds simple, but it is actually not easy, as human beings are far more disposed to be distracted by trivia – unnecessary interruptions, email, gossip, interesting asides, etc. Your brain would much prefer to do easy stuff and fights you when you need to focus on bigger, tougher issues – developing a plan, having a difficult conversation, making a hard choice, etc. But these are the sorts of things that move your business forward. In essence, you have to choose between being busy or being effective. Hopefully everything that is important to do today isn't just on the list because it has now become urgent owing to neglect!

Organise your day

Many of us unwittingly allow others to schedule our day. Over the years we have observed that it's much easier to do the harder stuff earlier in the day, as you are rested and your brain is not depleted. (The science backs this up, whether you think you are an early bird or a night owl!) So it makes sense to tackle the difficult stuff first, e.g. a difficult report you have to write, a conversation with a problem employee or client. In other words, arrange meetings with yourself to do the important work. If you allow others to interrupt or arrange early meetings for you, it is likely you will have run out of oomph and willpower by the time you get to this stuff. Guard your mornings, we say! Do the hard stuff first and the rest of the day is smooth sailing. Block off periods in your day for specific critical tasks and keep everything time bound, e.g. allow yourself ninety minutes to write a difficult report or thirty minutes to make x number of sales calls. Remember that your body needs rest often (every ninety minutes) and five minutes away from your desk walking around the block or perhaps with your headphones on listening to your favourite music will renew you for the next ninety minutes of hard work and help you to focus on planned activity. Keep your least productive time for routine stuff and things that don't require your 'best brain'. The important stuff must never be at the mercy of the trivial – it's your job to identify what's important to you and your business. Scheduling the important stuff in your diary will defend you from other people's demands and the chaos that is always threatening a business.

Check out or even disappear!

One of the reasons many businesses don't advance is because the leader never gets a chance to think about the bigger picture, review strategy, plan for the future, etc. Depending on your circumstances, this may be almost impossible at work – you may not be able to close the door, the environment is too hectic, or you work from home with all the attendant distractions. We have found it's really valuable to have a regular diarised time with yourself – take yourself to a café, a bench in the park, an empty room, the lobby of a nice hotel – wherever – and have some time out to think about the business. This allows you to store up issues you need to consider, or to get done the reading you need to do, or to plan a difficult conversation you have been putting off. It gets you out of the day-to-day and forces you to be strategic. Don't designate this a luxury; think of it as essential to your success – try doing it at the same time, same day every week so that you create a habit or ritual out of it. George Bernard

Shaw said that some folk only think once or twice a year, but that he had managed to make himself an international reputation by thinking once or twice a week!

Procrastinate – on the right stuff

The truth is we all procrastinate on some things. The thing that differentiates effective managers from all the rest is that they procrastinate on the less important stuff! Again the message is learn to identify what's most important. Accept that you will never get everything done. Procrastinate on the stuff that doesn't matter – forever, if necessary!

Take charge of the technology

Email, text messaging, mobile phones and other mobile devices have been fantastic for business – especially for smaller ones and those located in remote places. They enable us to do business anytime, anywhere. However, they have the potential to be very distracting, thereby reducing your effectiveness and productivity. If you are not careful these technologies can drive you, as opposed to you using them to make you successful. Because these technologies are immediate we are likely to find ourselves 'on and available' 24/7. This is highly ineffective and exhausting, and it takes away all our focus – instead of identifying and concentrating on what matters most, we respond to whatever calls. It's really important that you manage your communications: turn off the alert that tells you when you have a new email, put your phone on silent. Decide when is the best time to deal with your messages and restrict yourself to that. If you start your day with email you are likely to lose your best and freshest time reading unimportant stuff and being distracted by drivel. There is almost never anything urgent there – and if there is the person will find you. Keep message clearing time to a minimum. The end of the day is good as it won't derail your priorities and you have a big incentive to get finished and go. It's also a good time to call people, as they want to go too!

Forget multitasking

The brain can't do it; it can only oscillate fast between tasks with a lot of effort and a great loss of attention. Multitasking is a myth – unless you are doing stuff so mundane that it's automatic, like stirring a saucepan, wiping a toddler and giving homework help. (Well, mothers can!!) But don't kid yourself that you can do the difficult and crucial things you need to attend to in order to make your business a success any way other than one at a time. And 'attend' is the key word – your brain can only attend to one thing properly at a time. You may have multiple roles (e.g. entre-preneur, parent, partner, daughter, friend) and may have to wear multiple hats at times (in your business you may be owner, manager, employee and family member at any given moment), but at any point you should be attending to only one thing with a clear head.

Outsource where you can

You have lots of big, difficult, meaty stuff to do to make your business thrive. One of the most important things you must do is get others with the necessary skills, abilities and qualifications, etc., to do lots of things instead of you. We'll come back to the issue of delegation at work, but think about all of the stuff that has to be done but which need not be done by you – housework, childcare, shopping, gardening, present buying, cooking, etc. There is no intent here to tell you how to run your life, merely a stimulus to think about how you are spending your time. It usually takes a huge amount of time and energy to make a business grow and succeed and you can't do everything yourself. You are not a bad or inadequate person if you give away a lot of other tasks – you must if you are to succeed. If you yourself don't have to do a particular task and it doesn't fall into your category of things you love to do (or sometimes even if it does but someone being paid less than you could do it just as easily), then give your business a chance and get it off your own plate. Your job is to identify what tasks can and should go elsewhere. Contracting out administrative, technical or secretarial services to an independent 'virtual assistant' can be a great way of delegating tasks in a cost-effective way (if based in another continent they'll work while you're asleep!).

Get into the flow

Work – of any kind – gets a very bad press. On the other

hand we are never happier than when we are working hard, throwing ourselves entirely into things we really care about – walking hard in the mountains, keeping fit, making progress in our business, solving challenging problems, achieving our goals, playing with children, taking care of those we love. Plenty of research supports the idea that we are at our best and our happiest when fully absorbed in a particular task and working at the edge of our abilities. This is a priceless feeling and you should make the effort necessary to spend as much of your time in that state of flow as you can. You owe it to yourself and your business to be busy on worthwhile things and to prevent your flow of opportunities from being poisoned by frenzy.

Look after yourself – remember the basics

Good nutrition, regular exercise, sleep and adequate water intake are vital basics for everyone. Too often in our work we meet business owners working long hours with little or no rest periods during the day, poor exercise, sleep and eating habits. This is detrimental to long-term health as well as to the success of the business. You must take care of yourself if you want to be the best you can, reach your highest potential and build the best business possible.

Nobody gets all of this right all of the time, but it's worth making the effort to get it right more than you get it wrong.

Putting Pareto into Practice

Killer Questions

> *What's the 20% of my business that delivers 80% of the value?*
>
> *What are the 20% of issues that I need to focus my efforts on?*
>
> *What's in the 80% 'trivial many' that I can get rid of?*

Vilfredo Pareto was a nineteenth-century Italian economist and sociologist. He is justifiably famous because he showed that 80% of the wealth of the nation was distributed between only 20% of the population. Of course the remaining 20% of the wealth was all that the remaining 80% of people had to share. Relevant? Yes, because the ratio holds true in so many arenas. Pareto went on to show that 80% of land was owned by 20% of the population and so on.

We now talk about this principle as the 80/20 rule or the difference between the 'vital few' and the 'trivial many'. The basic principle suggests that in most normal situations we find that roughly 20% of the items account for 80% of the effect. This is a very powerful idea. It can provide a very useful principle for running your business and especially for the leveraging of your time, efforts and resources. The actual percentages may not always be precise, but it's the idea that is so useful – a minority of inputs produces a majority of outputs.

The resources of a small business and of its leader are limited. Often we feel overwhelmed by the amount of things that need to be tackled and the work that needs to be done. When your resources and energies are limited it pays to remember that frequently:

- *20% of your products/services account for 80% of your results.*

- *20% of your clients will be delivering 80% of your business.*

- *20% of your customers/suppliers/staff will be causing 80% of your problems!*

You could keep going in this vein. What about customer complaints, faulty products, lost time, insurance claims, etc.?

These insights should have clear implications for your efforts: your time, energies and resources need to go to the vital few, the things that if you get them right will deliver 80% of the value. It should help you identify very quickly where to direct your efforts, what problems you need to solve, which people you need to have conversations with, etc. This is a great way of getting rid of an overwhelming 'to do' list and also to prevent yourself being pulled hither and thither by the latest issue. It encourages us to analyse issues and assure ourselves we are spending nearly all of our time dealing with the vital few that will deliver the most value. The trivial many must be made to wait!

Focus

We have noticed in the course of the workshops we run that the best owner operators have wonderful focus. They are very clear about what is 'on top' for their business. They work very hard to isolate the few things that will make all the difference if they resolve them, e.g. developing a clear plan, finding great people to work with them, refining their business model until it hums, paying attention to key clients, etc. It's hard to distract them with trivia: they don't allow others to steal their day and they don't wait to decide what to do until they check their email. Great operators have great focus because they instinctively understand Pareto's Law, even if they have never heard of him. They are also the ones that always ensure they get holidays and adequate time away from the business!

Don't Just Do It – Delegate It!

Killer Question

> *What's the long-term impact on you and your business if you don't delegate?*

Many business owners have strong tendencies towards 'do it yourself'. This is understandable and admirable – after all, without these instincts you would be unlikely to ever set up in business yourself. However, there is a negative side to this trait – we see a great deal of systematic under-delegation. This is very wasteful in many ways: the business owner is doing things that others could do and at the same time is too busy to do things that only the person in that position may be able to do. Staff are frustrated because of lack of development and responsibility, and the better ones often leave in search of more challenging work. The boss is often acting as a bottleneck, preventing the business from moving forward.

What stops you delegating?

There are many reasons why business owners fail to

delegate. It's important to know what stops you so that you can change and unleash the real potential in your business.

Some barriers are self-imposed:

- I prefer 'doing' to managing/leading because I understand it better.
- I can do the work better than they can.
- I don't know how to delegate.
- It is easier and quicker to do it myself.
- We can't afford any mistakes.

Sometimes we blame the people around us for our lack of delegation:

- My employees lack experience.
- My employees are overloaded.
- My employees resist responsibility.
- My employees avoid risk.

Sometimes we blame the situation:

- Clients expect me to do important things personally.
- My employees can't be trusted to work on their own.
- We are under-staffed.

Whatever your excuse, under-delegation needs to be sorted out as it will choke your business and prevent it from growing.

The 'why?' of delegation

Sometimes we assign a low priority to delegation because we are unsure of how to go about it and may be overwhelmed by the situation we find our business in. The following are some of the benefits of delegating: which of these would you like to achieve for yourself and your business?

- More can be achieved – deadlines are easier to meet.
- Employees become more involved and committed.
- The assignment of specific authority and responsibility makes control less difficult.
- Employees grow and develop.
- People are better utilised and there is greater productivity.
- Individual performance can be measured more accurately.
- Compensation can be more directly related to individual performance.
- A diversity of products, operations and people can be managed effectively.
- Distant operations can be managed with less travel and stress.

- Employee recognition and satisfaction can be enhanced.
- The manager has time for planning, organising, motivating and monitoring.
- The manager has time for leading: communicating, conversing, developing and nurturing great people.

How to delegate

We think that most business owners fail to delegate because they just don't know how to go about it well. That means that they often try, get burned and give up. You can optimise your chances of delegation working well by adopting a structured approach. It's a good idea to develop a simple template based on the headings below. If you set this up, fill it in each time and discuss it with your employee (or get them to complete it after your briefing to show you that they have fully understood it), then you have a high chance of success. The time taken to do this far outweighs the time you will have to spend if the task is not done properly.

Why?

- Why is the delegated task important?
- Why is the task being delegated in the first place?
- Why to that particular person?

What?

- What should be achieved at the end?
- What are the desired results?

Who?

- Who are the parties involved?

How?

- What are any guidelines you want to specify?
- What are the limits of authority, e.g. what can you commit us to?
- How much money or time can be spent?

Support and assistance

- Who can be called on if help is required?
- What resources can be used to do the job?
- What checking in needs to happen?

When?

- What timelines need to be followed?
- When must it be finished?

Feedback

- What feedback needs to be solicited to ensure the person fully understands the task?

Remember to tell others who are affected that the task has been delegated and that you have given the person authority to act on your behalf – this may be especially important if you have delegated things to a PA or a new/junior person who is not usually so empowered.

Making it happen

Your first job is to consider what can be delegated. It's often easier to make a list of what cannot be delegated e.g.:

- Tasks beyond the skills of others.
- Confidential and security matters.
- Disciplinary matters.

You should be able to come up initially with a list of:

- Routine tasks.
- Time-consuming tasks.

Consider the candidates for delegation. And remember, they do not need to be employees. As many small businesses just don't have anyone to delegate to, consider getting help from family, friends and college interns. You may wish to contract out some work, or may want to use an agency or a virtual assistant for some tasks:

- Who has time?
- Who is ready for new challenges?
- What training will be needed?

Then, using your template, set the delegation in motion:

- Define the task in writing.
- Establish the problems and the pitfalls of the task.
- Define any additional authority needed.
- Establish the authority.
- Explain the task, its pitfalls and its good points.
- Go through the task with those who are to undertake it.
- Set report-back targets for everyone involved.

Then monitor, which means standing back and watching, not taking over. Remember, there's no one in the world who wants a micro-manager for their boss!

Achieving Your Financial Freedom

Killer Questions

> *Why are you in business?*
> *What's the endgame?*
> *What do you want to be and what do you want to be doing
>   in ten years time?*

What is financial freedom?

Financial freedom is that happy state where both your money and your time are your own. Your money is your own in the sense that you have low or no borrowings; your time is your own in that you no longer need to drive your business hard on a daily basis.

There are plenty of people who are wealthy but are not financially free. These people have very valuable businesses and therefore have high net worth, but they are still carrying large debts and the owners are still working many hours a week. Financial freedom means having security assets that will give you sufficient income to live the life that you want without risk and with little work. The business should make you wealthy, but you need to be thinking of the endgame – and for most people the endgame is financial freedom.

It starts with a dream!

Unfocused activity rarely leads anywhere good. Start thinking about what you really want in life. Many people who own their own business lose sight of why they set it up and why they are working so hard. What is it that you really, *really* want in life? Get as specific as you can. Ask yourself (and your partner) questions like:

- What would we do with our lives if we won the Lottery?
- What would we do if we only had a year to live?
- What would an ideal year in my life look like?
- How would I like to live?
- What do I want to have in my life?
- Who do I want to be?
- What things would I like to do before I die?
- What is my purpose in life? Why am I here?

Dreams

Use these questions as prompts to discover what you yearn for. When you are clear about what you really want it is much easier to set about doing what you need to do to make the dream a reality – that's where the energy comes from. Write it down or draw it or paint a picture

… and decide you are going to have it! Why shouldn't everyone have the life of his or her dreams?

Cost your dreams

The next step is to work out what it would take for you to live the life of your dreams. The clearer you are about your dream the easier it is to cost it. How much money would you need to do and become whatever you want? How much would you need as income each year to live the life you are describing? When you have worked this out you know your goals – this is the amount of wealth you need to create through your business so that you can stop working (any more than you want to) and live the dream life.

Properly invested in security assets, your wealth should give you a real return of around 6–8% per annum before tax (on good assets over the long term). So if you determine that you need €80,000 a year in income before tax, then you will need about €1m (in addition to a home) in order to fund your dream life.

Do some sums. The dream life is often not as expensive or as far away as you may think. And set some dates

– how many years will you need to achieve this amount
– maybe you can do it now!

Where are you at?

How much wealth do you have right now? Where are you starting from? Your net worth is the sum of your wealth if you were to cash in everything today – sell the business, the house and any other assets, and repay any debts that you might have such as a mortgage or a loan to the business. Do a net worth statement: list all of your assets and all of your liabilities (debts). Your net worth is the sum of your assets minus the sum of your liabilities. Don't bother counting assets such as sports equipment, cars, boats or jewellery unless they are very valuable – they just clutter up your calculations and they usually sell for very little no matter how dear they are to you!

Net Worth

Assets	Value	Liability
House		
Business		
Property		
Shares		
Pension Funds		
Cash		
Deposits		
Other		

Totals

Sample Net Worth

Assets	Value	Liability
House	€350,000	€200,000
Business	€500,000	€100,000
Property	€200,000	€120,000
Shares	€20,000	
Pension Funds	€30,000	
Cash		
Deposits		
Other		

Totals	*€1,100,000*	*(€420,000)*
Net Worth	*€680,000*	

When you have done your net worth statement you will know how big the gap you have to close is. If the couple in the example above need €1m in addition to their home for financial freedom, then they will need to create about €670,000 more wealth at today's values.

Planning is everything

When you are clear about your dream – the endgame – and know how much wealth you need to create, the next step is to do a plan to get you from here to there. You have to close the gap between your current net worth and the amount you need for the dream.

The key question the business owner must ask is whether the business is capable of providing this wealth. Can you grow your business to close the gap between where you are and where you need to be for financial freedom?

Will your business give you the dream?

Now, you need to look hard at your business and ask these four questions:

1. Does your business model make money?

2. Can your business grow over the next few years to be worth the amount you need?

3. Will you be able to develop it so that it can be sold for the value that you want to fund your dream life?

4. If it won't be a saleable business in the future (and many are not), can it throw off enough income over the next few years so that you can invest in other things (such as shares, managed funds) to create the wealth you need?

If the answer to all of these is 'NO' then why are you in this business? Are you just self-employed and creating a job for yourself – one that you will never sell or make additional money from? You may be fishing in a 'dry ditch' – some industries and some businesses have little wealth potential. In other words, you may be wasting your time and energies – and no matter how hard you work, the business you are in may have little potential. If that is the case, do yourself a favour (unless you like working hard for little reward) and get out now. Before you give up, however, have a look at the chapter 'Developing a Stronger Business Model' (see page 100) for some ideas on how you might be able to adapt your business.

To become wealthy enough to have financial freedom you must have a 'wealth-creating asset'. This asset (hopefully your business) is either generating enough cash or growing enough capital to make you wealthy enough to be free sometime in the future.

Don't play double or quits ... business is risky!

Every business owner thinks that their business will be a success, but the evidence says differently. Look at how many businesses go under and how few are still around five years after they open. Look at how many struggle along, barely surviving, but giving no proper return on the owner's time and capital. That should not put you off, but it should make you very clear-headed.

The purpose of the business is to create value and capital. Don't reinvest everything back in the business! So many business owners put all their profits back into the business by buying more plant and equipment, increasing stock levels, opening a new division, etc. If you do this, you are risking everything on your next decision – a new product, extra staff, a new store – any of these could turn sour and take everything you have got and put you out of the game. Of course you have to take risks in business – but don't gamble *everything* on the next throw of the dice. You are playing 'double or quits' if you reinvest everything in the business and you have given the bank a mortgage over your home to fund it all. Therefore, it is vital that you invest outside the business as well as in the business.

Where to stash your cash

Many business owners get very rich – for a while! Not so many remain rich. On paper some are worth millions but because of the way business – and life – operates, it could all disappear. Business creates wealth – but security assets store wealth. Security assets are assets you own that have no (or little) debt – in other words they are largely insulated from a rise in rates or a downturn in the markets. Likewise, they are not high risk because you are not seeking high returns but rather security. The secret to staying rich and achieving financial freedom, so that you can have the life you want, is to get some of your wealth out of the business and into more secure assets. Business is a great wealth creator but your business is not a safe place for all your wealth. You cannot afford to leave all of your wealth in the business until you are ready to sell – you could lose it all in a moment. You may not have the time or energy left to rebuild. So start early and get some wealth out as you go, difficult though that may be. Don't let a slavish devotion to the cash needs of the business interfere with sound investment principles. It's your life – and your dreams – that are at stake!

Moreover, your money should be spread around. A diversified range of investments is the safest place for your money. This works on the principle that all investments show fluctuations and go up and down. A spread of investments takes away much of the risk so that all of your eggs are not in the same basket. So you don't want all of your money in one country, you don't want all of your shares in one company and you certainly don't want all of your wealth in one company – your own!

What may MAKE you wealthy	What will KEEP you wealthy
• a business • highly-leveraged property • an aggressive share portfolio	• a diversified portfolio (e.g. property, shares and deposits) • un-leveraged property • widely spread shares • pension funds • bonds

How people become wealthy – or broke!

People growing wealth rejoice when their wealth-creating assets (business or property or shares) show growth in income. The increased income means the asset has a higher value and allows them to take on additional borrowings that they reinvest to generate further income … and repeat the cycle. This can work brilliantly well – or spin out of control! Then it becomes a vicious spiral into bankruptcy. Understand the risks and take steps to move some of your wealth into security assets.

The Virtuous Circle of Wealth

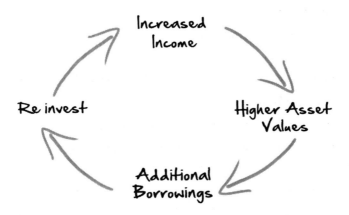

What about the returns from security assets?

You may well be getting a very good return on your money in your own business and so think it is the best place to invest. While you may be outperforming a diversified portfolio, the whole point of investing elsewhere is to lower the risk. Anywhere there are high returns there is high risk – and that includes the business! A diversified portfolio won't give high returns – but you are unlikely to lose all your money. The whole point of investing outside your business is for security – and so that you will assure yourself of passive income in the future.

Are you getting a return on your time?

Many business owners work for nothing. Not only do they not pay themselves a proper salary or wage from the business, but they don't even count the value of their time. Why does this matter (after all, it's their business)? Let's say your expertise and skills are worth €60,000 p.a. on the open market but you do not pay yourself that in your business. Your business made a 'profit' last year of €80,000 and you think that is very good and are proud. Wrong! Your business made a €20,000 profit and is therefore not worth much if you wanted to sell it. Your profit statement is misrepresenting the profitability of the business.

To build wealth to fund your dream you need to think very clearly about whether you are getting a return on your time from the business as well as a return on the capital you have invested (and risked) in your business.

Take action!

Now that you know what you want (dreams), and have

costed your dreams (goals) and know what you need to do to make the dream a reality (plan) you must ACT!

You have to Act!

NETWORKING –
IT'S WHO YOU KNOW

Winners have wide networks

Successful business people have good networks. They know what is going on in their industry and in their locality. They have a feel for what is happening in their market because they are out and about talking to others in the know. They get encouragement and support from their network – and maybe even referrals and recommendations. It is very hard to succeed without a network that is appropriate to your business. Knowing *what* and knowing *how* are important; knowing *who* is essential.

Killer Questions

Your net worth will be largely determined by your network – how powerful is your network?

How often do you work at your network?

When you network online, what are other's perceptions of you?

Mapping your network

EXERCISE

- Diagram or mind map your existing network (family, friends, relatives, business contacts).

- Map in the other key people that these people know.

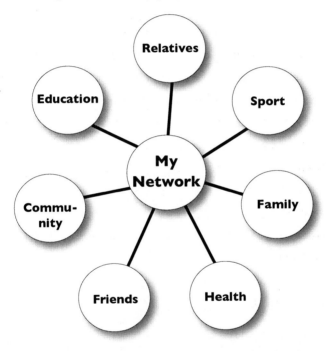

- Identify the gaps in your network, e.g. do you know people who know the latest about what is going on in your industry, what is happening at local government level that could affect your business, what is concerning your customers, etc.

- Figure out who you would need to know or have access to in order to be more up to date with the information you need to keep your business a success.

Peopling your map

Get busy on building your network and filling in the gaps. Everyone knows someone who knows someone who knows the information you want to find out, or knows the people you want to meet or reach. The more people who are in your network the more powerful it is. Look in all of the following groups to expand your net:

- family, relatives, in-laws
- friends and acquaintances
- children's friends and families
- former employers and colleagues
- current colleagues and staff
- school and college friends and classmates
- church and parish members
- health professionals – doctors, nurses, dentists
- advisers – accountants, lawyers, risk specialists, brokers
- consultants – sales, marketing, business
- community leaders and local politicians
- industry and local trade groups

- sports clubs, gym, fellow joggers
- customers, suppliers
- other business people.

You can reach anyone!

Stanley Milgram, a Yale University psychologist, showed in 1967 that you could reach anyone in the world in about six steps. He devised an experiment where people had to send a package to a stranger via acquaintances they knew well. On average it took about five intermediaries to reach a complete stranger. This became famously known as the 'six degrees of separation'. No one is beyond the reach of you/your business!

Clubs and associations

Everything from sports clubs to service organisations (e.g. Rotary) to general business associations (e.g. Chamber of Commerce) or established networks for entrepreneurs (such as those started by the City and County Enterprise Boards and Skillnets) are good places for meeting the people who can help with your business. Most industries have specialised associations that will be of use to your business. You can also form your own. Small informal groups work very well also, e.g. a group of business people with similar interests and challenges who might meet for a monthly lunch or have a designated evening each week for an after-work drink.

Ten checks for choosing a good networking association

1. What's the association for – does it meet your needs?
2. Does it serve your area/industry well?
3. Can its members help you learn and grow personally?
4. Can its members help you learn and grow professionally?
5. Does it meet often enough?
6. Does it meet at a time that works for you?
7. Has it got good processes and routines?
8. Can you *present* your business to the group?
9. Can you arrive early/stay late for informal networking?
10. Can you join now?

Working the room

All of us do this at every family and social event. The better you are at it the more you will enjoy sport, church and community involvement. People are very uncomfortable with strangers so the trick is to learn how not to be with 'strangers' as fast as possible. Learn to be with and enjoy people in as many environments as possible and the business benefits will follow. You can master mingling by:

- **Introducing yourself** – '*I'm Joan and I'm here because Michael is my son ...*', '*I'm Jack and I have just moved here from ...*'

- **Asking questions** – *'Who else do you know here?', 'What started your interest in …?', 'How do you know …?'*

- **Making connections** – *'Can I introduce you to …?', 'Would you introduce me to …?'*

- **Taking action** – *'May I get you a drink?', 'Who don't you know?'*

Behave like a host not a guest

If you are shy or have been taught that it is rude to approach those you don't know or interrupt conversations uninvited, you may be inclined to hover uncomfortably at the edges of the crowd and seek the earliest escape. Everyone feels like this when confronted with a room of strangers, but the smart ones have better strategies for dealing with their discomfort. Guests tend to behave passively waiting to be introduced, invited to join in, expect to be offered food and drink or be rescued. The problem is that you may be perceived as cold, indifferent or standoffish rather than shy. The best strategy is to behave as if you were a host:

- *'Hi, I'm Jim. Who are you?*

- With plate of food: *'Have one of these – they are delicious. I'm Mike…'*

- *'May I take your coat?'*

- *'What will you have to drink?'*

- *'Did you come alone? Would you like to circulate with me?'*

Networking online

There are a huge number of opportunities to network online, starting with LinkedIn, Facebook, Twitter and many discussion boards. When you network online, be clear about the persona you want to project. To build up your profile you can strike up conversations about topics of interest to your business and industry, give answers to questions and ask questions. Online networking will help to build your online brand (discussed further on pages 191–3).

Networking relationships: hard networking v. soft networking

Many people are uncomfortable with the idea of networking as they think that it is just about selling. It may help to think about the different attitudes that people bring. Some certainly do wish to sell and make no secret of it. Many others are looking for a relationship that may offer information, support, personal development, a sense of community and even true friendship over time.

If both of you simply want to sell you may be able to do a deal that benefits each of you. There is nothing wrong with this – after all, all business is a deal. If you are seeking some form of relationship but encounter others who simply want to sell, you may need to be careful that you are not taken advantage of and simply get done over! On the other hand, you need to be careful of exploiting others' generosity – it is never good for your business to be seen to exploit contacts you have made. People don't like people on the make. It takes time, but the best strategy for you and your business is to develop relationships with as many people as you can. The emphasis should be on win-win – make sure that you give as well as get. If at all possible, give *before* you take and give *more* than you take.

Business cards – the best (and cheapest) tool!

If you don't already carry business cards then get some printed. They can be as simple as you like – just name and contact details. They make it much easier to exchange contact details with others and give you a record and reminder of those you have met. Collect as many as you can – you never know when you will want to contact someone again. Take cards with you wherever you go. It helps you later if you make a note on the cards you collect of where you met the person.

Maximise the effectiveness of cards:

- Make sure your name, business and phone number are easy to read.

- Photos work well to remind people of you.

- Decide how you will carry and use them at events – e.g. use one pocket for yours and another to collect cards.

- File those you collect by event or type.

- Write on them – something to remember the person by.

- Always have some of yours with you.

- Keep them in good condition for a good impression.

- Get yours professionally designed.

- Consider double-sided or folding cards to carry additional information about your business.

Network with a purpose

It's a good idea before each networking opportunity to have clear objectives and purposes in mind. A target keeps you focused and helps you avoid wasting time. If you are shy or uncomfortable, a specific purpose for the occasion will help you forget about yourself. It also gets you to measure your own networking behaviour and how effective you are being. These objectives can be personal or professional or a mixture of both. Targets you set might include:

- Having fun.

- Meeting new people.

- Making new friends.

- Learning something about yourself.

- Learning something about business/industry/locality.

- Feeling more confident about socialising/networking.

- Learning about other people's businesses.

- Increasing your business.

- Practising one new networking skill, e.g. playing 'host'.

- Finding someone who knows someone who ...

Following up

What's next? After you have made a new contact you may want to consolidate the meeting. Consider what's appropriate:

- Send an email – 'thanks for the chat, looking forward to meeting again'.

- Make a phone call – ditto.

- Organise a coffee or a lunch.

- Send a brochure about your business.

- Clip an article or send a magazine that is relevant.

- Make an invitation to visit your business.

- Offer a helping hand to someone you met.

Rules for smart networkers

1. **Don't be greedy** – people don't like people on the make.

2. **Be a giver rather than a taker** – help someone before you help yourself.

3. **Know why you are there** – be honest and up-front about what you want.

4. **Know who is in your network** – who can you call for what.

5. **Invest your time well** – don't waste time with those who can't/won't help.

6. **Nurture your network** – keep in touch with those you already know.

7. **Be trustworthy** – trust is at the heart of all relationships.

Love the ones you're with!

Don't be a Casanova chasing after new loves when you already have a good love. Some people simply rack up 'names' or drop associates as soon as someone more interesting comes along. Successful businesses are a marathon not a sprint. It is very important that you treat people properly and with respect. The success of your business rests on building and strengthening relationships with those you already know – and you know a lot more people than you think you do! Ask yourself if you are seeing enough of clients, suppliers, business associates, advisers and business neighbours. Love the ones you are already involved with by:

- Knowing their names.
- Greeting them with warmth.
- Remembering them with Christmas cards, etc.
- Helping them where you can.

Seminars and events

If you attend a seminar, course or conference on a topic of interest to your business, you are highly likely to meet business people with similar issues and interests. These people can broaden your network throughout the country, internationally and into other industries. Many will not be in competition with you and so may be very generous with their help – offering the opportunity to visit other premises or meet experts in your field.

Your Sounding Board

The company you keep really matters. It is a mistake to think that you can do everything yourself – no one has all of the skills, never mind the time and energy. The people you surround yourself with have a great influence on the success of your business. The better informed you are the better the quality of your decisions. Owners of small businesses can be very isolated – having good people to consult with and to challenge you is essential to success.

Killer Questions

> *Are your advisers good enough to take you and your business where you want to go?*
> *Are your advisers as good as your competitors' advisers?*

Assembling a 'dream team' of professionals

Ultimately it's your business, but you don't have to do it all alone. There are lots of people who can help in any industry. No matter how good you are at whatever you do you will need expert help from time to time. If you are committed to making your business grow and succeed you should surround yourself with a 'dream team' of professionals who can assist you with expert advice and help in making decisions about your business.

And you need good people. Winners work with winners – you need people who are winners in their own professions. You also need a *team*. Professionals and experts are often jealous of each other's expertise and influence. You need them to work together in the interests of *your business.*

Depending on your business you will need one or more of the following from time to time:

- accountant
- legal adviser
- risk adviser
- tax specialist
- investment adviser
- succession planner
- business consultant
- business broker
- marketing consultant
- HR consultant
- IT consultant.

Get a heavyweight

No matter how good you are at what you do, or how hard you work, you cannot expect to be an expert in all the areas of expertise that your business may need. You will need to access external advice. And you need *good* advice – when the going gets tough you need to be able to call on a heavyweight in the appropriate field.

If you don't already have a team for your business, you should start to build your team of advisers as soon as possible. Just as with a medical professional, you don't want to be meeting these people for the first time on a day of crisis. Neither do you want to be selecting them from the phone book – rather you want to build a team by reputation and reference from others you trust. Winners *do* work with winners – ask the best you know in any field to recommend those in other fields. A good accountant can point to the best legal adviser. A good general business consultant will be able to recommend the better marketing and HR professionals.

If you think dealing with a professional is expensive try dealing with an amateur ...

The level of professional you need depends on your business and circumstances. If your business affairs are very straightforward a junior or inexperienced person may be competent enough. Always remember, however, that your business is competing with someone who is getting good advice! The problem with cheaper/less experienced people is that they do not know what they do not know. Remember that poor advice is the most expensive money you will ever spend. It's not what you pay, it's the value you get that matters.

Professional fees

Business people often complain about professional fees. However, there are several things you can do to minimise professional fees:

- Keep your advisers informed so that they don't spend lots of time (and your money!) finding out what they should have already known/been told by you.

- Get organised. Make sure that all of the documentation they need is available and that they can talk to the people in your business that they need to see. Be available – you'll be charged for wasting their time.

- Do what you can yourself. For example, many businesses use accountants to do things they could easily do themselves (e.g. VAT returns, cash flow forecasts). Often the professional is adding nothing that you don't know – except their time and that costs!

- Negotiate a preset price. It is perfectly acceptable to ask for a quote or to establish a cap on fees for an assignment or to contract only on a stage-by-stage basis. You could also negotiate an annual fee for specified services and meetings. This makes your budgeting and cash flow easier to manage.

Don't assume you always have to go to the traditional sources for advice: some associations and bodies representing your industry can provide very valuable advice to add to the mix.

Get them working as a team

Success is a team game and you need to make sure that your group of advisers work *together* in the interests of your business. First you need to assemble the team you need; then you need to get them to work together. All too often advisers have a relationship only with the owner/manager. They can tend to countermand each other's advice and compete with each other for the ear of the owner.

Some ways to get them working as a team include:

- Get them together from time to time, e.g. when you are planning or have a big issue to resolve or even for a social occasion.

- Encourage them to deal directly with each other, e.g. suggesting to the legal adviser that he have a word with the accountant about some matter without you needing to be in the middle. You can authorise this in writing if any of the parties have professional scruples about discussing your business in your absence.

- Insist that they keep each other informed – don't allow them to use you as an 'in-basket'. Ensure that communication flows in all directions as in the diagram.

- Circulate pertinent information to all of them – give them no excuse to be uninformed or to play off against each other.

- Be clear in your expectations that they work as a team in the interests of your business.

- Don't hesitate to remove an adviser who is not a team

player. Everyone will respect you for this and take the team approach even more seriously.

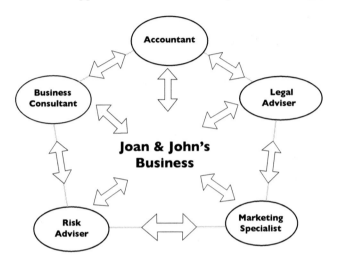

Ultimately you are in charge. You can hire the best and delegate authority to them. But it's your business and you can't assume that advisers will now take care of everything. You will need to be firm in your expectations of performance in order to get the best from your team of advisers.

Are you getting the best?

How do you know what to ask for? We often only understand the value we have received in hindsight. It can be very difficult to work out what you should be able to expect from the different professionals and advisers you use. The table below is a guide to the types of services that can be expected. You should use it to evaluate what you are getting now and to plan to get the most from your team of advisers.

Profession	Usual services	Should be able to advise on	Ideally provides
Accountant	Accounts Tax returns Forecasts Audits	Business structures Business issues Tax Debt Due diligence	Advice on planning for changes, e.g. growth of business Tax minimisation Business advice
Solicitor/ Legal adviser	Company formation Court represen-tation Trust formation Contracts Terms of trade Leases Wills	Business structures Trust management Succession planning IP protection Due diligence Buy/sell agreements Employment issues	Updates to wills Notice of anticipated changes in legislation Business advice
Financial adviser	Insurance Investments	Investments Debt management Financial plans	A highly customised plan On-going guidance Proactive commu-nication on changes which may affect you
Business broker	Buy business Sell business	Business value The market for businesses	Services needed to buy or sell a business
Estate agent	Agreements for sale or purchase of property Leasing	Trends Where the market is	Updates on property in your area of interest Updates on the market

Business consultant	General business advice	Some speciality, e.g. marketing	Conduit to other experts Advice on direction of business Valued sounding board
Stockbroker	Sale or purchase of shares, investments	Recommendations for sale/purchase of investments Listings of new companies Bond issues Research	Priority for new listings Ongoing advice/ research on companies of interest
Risk adviser	Insurance	Buy/sell agreements Risk management	Regular review of your risk profile Risk mitigation strategies

Tips for choosing advisers

- Use your network to find people who will suit you, your business and your issues. Word of mouth recommendations from people who you know and can trust are always best.

- Reference check the people you are considering. Speak to other clients and check what kind of work they have done. Be sure to ask about their people skills as you will want them to work as a team player.

- Interview prospective advisers and try to establish how well they understand your type of business and business issues. Check how up to date their information is in their field – are they keeping up with their profession by reading, attending seminars and participating in professional networks?

- Find out if they are 'strong' enough for you. Most entrepreneurs are strong willed and used to running the show. But you don't need an echo! Check that the adviser has the competence, the professional integrity and the personal resilience to challenge you when it is needed. Are they good enough to tell you when you are wrong? That's what you are paying for.

- Ask about their fees and how they are paid. This is also something to check with referees. High hourly rates will not be a problem if you are dealing with somebody who is competent and efficient and who actually delivers. You can establish how you wish to pay and on what basis right from the start.

Help them be great

It's in your interest to make sure that it is as easy as possible for advisers to give you what your business needs. Help them get it right:

- Brief them well. Be clear about the results you want. If possible commit your expected results to paper.

- Give thorough information about your company background. Give them as much information as you can about the company and the relevant issues.

- Be specific. Set targets and deadlines.

- Use a dashboard of performance indicators – a good adviser will be happy to set them up together with you.

- Have regular meetings. Be available for consultation and ask for interim reports.

Do you need a board?

Your business does not have to have a formal board of directors unless you are taking it public. Many businesses choose to have a board anyway in order to introduce the disciplines that a board can bring. Your board can include appointed directors (who have legal powers, duties and liabilities under the Companies Act, 1963) or could consist of a group of advisers, professionals, other family members and friends who act as an informal sounding board for you and the business. Board members may or may not be paid. The advantages of having a board (formal or just a sounding board) include the disciplines of:

- regular meetings
- minutes
- setting agendas
- reporting to the group
- exposure to a wide range of informed and interested viewpoints.

It is very easy for a small business to bypass these disciplines – there never seems to be enough time and you are often only answerable to yourself. A board, however informal, is a way of instituting some better business practices. People are usually flattered to be asked to be part of a sounding or advisory board for your business and it's a great way to avail of the knowledge, experience and wisdom of people you know. Depending on your business you could consider some relatively young members (to get different generational viewpoints), people from a different industry, politically astute people or those who are well connected in the community. Many retired businesspeople and professionals would be delighted to help in this not-too-onerous capacity.

Although most CEOs of small businesses don't appoint a formal board, serious consideration should be given to selecting and appointing what we term 'The Board You Can't Afford'. This is a group of six to ten entrepreneurs who can challenge and advise you in your business in a confidential setting. We facilitate many of these boards and have seen this work extremely well in practice and it can provide opportunities in the following ways:

- Huge learning opportunities for the participating businesses.
- Increased networking.
- Sales and new business opportunities.
- Mentoring and coaching for you and your business.
- A trustworthy sounding board, the like of which would be difficult to afford on the open market.

SECTION 2:
ORGANISATION

It's all too easy as a business owner to focus on the actual work you do for the business (e.g. sales, writing proposals, making presentations, presenting products, etc.) rather than on the total enterprise. That's not surprising, as you probably have a full-time job in the business trying to keep it going and get stuff out the door. The problem is that there is likely to be no one working full-time on the business. And that's your job!

There are so many bigger things that have to be taken care of – strategic direction, planning, modifying your business model, putting good controls in place, monitoring performance, etc., that you must attend to if your business is to thrive. Remember, running a business is about creating value and employment for others both internal and external to your business (extra work for suppliers, etc.). If you decide not to focus on this you will be reduced to just creating a job for yourself and not a wealth-creating asset.

Some of the most important things your business needs you to attend to are covered in this section.

CLARIFYING YOUR
BUSINESS DREAMS

Why does it matter? Doesn't that sort of thing belong to big corporations with vision statements plastered on the wall and which can fund expensive off-site conferences to ponder such things?

The simple answer is that it is important for you, no matter what the size of your business, to consider its ultimate goals. Why? Because it will help you to have a clearer view about what you are trying to achieve for the future. Your vision for the business is a positive image of what the organisation could become. The more attractive, the more compelling your vision is, the more power it has to focus you and to help you make the right choices and take the actions that you need to bring the vision closer.

The best businesses may start small but they have a big idea – they want to make a better world or in some way to offer people a better tomorrow. They look at the world as it is and ask why it cannot be better – why can't we have a better product or service in some area? They notice how people live, the challenges they face and the inadequacies of current offerings and they set out to provide something better. Ryanair set out to provide cheap travel for everyone – to democratise air travel. That's the big idea and they have made it work in a very difficult industry. We mentioned dreams briefly in Section 1, but we go into more detail here as to how and why you need to use them in your business.

Dreaming on

The best businesses are the best because someone has a vision – they want to create something that didn't exist, they want to build something that works, they want to provide a service that people need, they want to make something happen. Questions, therefore, arise for you. Have you a dream or a vision for your business? What do you want to create? How good could it be? What could you build that would make you proud?

There is, as we've already mentioned, much nonsense talked about business vision. You yourself may know of businesses that have vision and mission statements hanging on every available surface that no-one believes and that the organisation doesn't live up to.

However, there is a great kernel of valuable insight in the concept of the realistic business vision or mission – because people crave meaning and a raison d'être, something to aspire to and to strive for. As the business owner or leader, you need a clear view of what you are trying to build, what you want to attain. Everyone who works in the business needs to know why they are giving so much of their lives to your business – and a pay cheque isn't enough! We all want to know what our efforts are for. This sense of meaning is where your (and everyone's) energy comes from.

So ask yourself (and others in the business):

- How could we be great?
- How could we grow our business?
- What could we do to be 'best in class'?
- What do we want to be famous for?

So what's your own vision? What do you wish for yourself and for your business? It's OK to be a bit 'pie-in-the-sky' at this point, but what do you really want to achieve? This should be meaningful for you – after all, it's going to take a lot of your life and for much of it may be just hard work and very little profit. It had better matter to you! Ideally you should have a good sense of what people may be missing in their lives (e.g. great healthy food at lunchtime, better after-school care for their kids, family-friendly holiday experiences) and a sense that you could plug this need for your market or in your area.

Once you get this right you provide a lot of meaning to all your efforts. Likewise you provide meaning for the people who work with you – they understand why they need to do whatever it is they have to do. People are inspired when their work is meaningful – even if they are still carrying out very mundane tasks. The most basic of work is meaningful when you inspire others with meaning and vision.

When you know what the dream is, you can get busy making it happen.

Articulating your mission

Killer Question

What business are you in?

The term 'mission' may sound like jargon that has little or no place in a smaller business. That's not so – the trick for any business is to take the best ideas you can find anywhere and use them in a way that works for the business you have. One such best idea is that of the mission statement.

The *core idea* behind a mission statement is to state clearly what your business is or does. Nothing may seem simpler or more obvious – after all, a training business is about training, a catering business about food, a financial services business provides financial services. But asking, 'What is my business?' is almost always a penetrating question and the answer is often not that obvious at all.

The mission or purpose of your business is actually defined by the customer need it serves, not by the name of the business or the industry it is in. Your mission is to satisfy the customer in some particular way. To understand that, you have to stand outside your business and look at things from the customer's point of view. What is it that the client needs or wants? What problem are you solving? How is it that you make their lives better or easier?

To become really clear about the mission you serve you have to understand the customer very well. Working in this area helps you refine and clarify your mission over time so that you have a sweet spot where you meet a very well-identified need.

You don't have to craft a mission statement, much less get it on a marble plaque for your reception area. But you do need to know what the precise purpose of your business (or each individual business unit or revenue stream) is. And if you have other people working with you it is important that they understand too – after all, they will be making decisions, large or small, all day that affect how well your business is fulfilling its mission. They deserve to know why the business exists and how they can have influence in achieving that purpose. We look at this question in more detail later, when we talk about the planning process (see page 116).

Three Business Strategies for Success

Creating a business that creates wealth and freedom differentiates the business owner from the self-employed person – they have a business, not a job. People who do this usually follow one of three strategies:

1. Develop a valuable business and sell it.
2. Develop a business that can deliver profits without you.
3. Develop a business that generates big cash flows and suck them out.

1. Develop a valuable business and sell it

The strategy here is to build a sound business with a view to someone buying you out in the future. You will of course want to make good profits along the way (so the business can pay you a salary and dividends), but you will also want to create a lot of goodwill. Goodwill is the 'extra' that a buyer will be willing to pay for your business, rather than starting from scratch in competition with you or having to go through the same learning curve. Goodwill may be created through your reputation, your great team, your loyal customers, your wonderful locations and many other intangibles. It is the premium that you get from goodwill that will make you wealthy.

EXAMPLE

Petra developed her design and printing business from a small start. Over the years she accumulated a growing list of clients owing to her high standards of design and professional operations and delivery. She reinvested heavily in the business – there was little choice as technology advances meant that her equipment became rapidly obsolete. The market continued to change as people demanded ever-higher levels of design. Many businesses wanted short print runs that could be met with new and fast digital copying. Petra expanded her operation into nearby towns so ended up managing several staff over a wide geographical location. Her business reputation or brand was very good and competitors would have needed to make a very big investment to compete head on where she was already established. There are high barriers to entry in that industry as there is considerable capital investment in plant and equipment as well as skilled labour.

One of the big names in the industry made Petra an offer she couldn't refuse – they wanted to dominate that territory and she was in the way. They judged it far easier to buy her out than invest the several years of effort and investment it would take to grab her market share. Petra is now 'retired' (reading, travelling, thinking of starting another business, playing with her grandchildren) with enough wealth to live the life of her dreams.

2. Develop a business that can deliver profits without you

This strategy requires you to develop a business to a size and level of success that allows you to install professional management to continue to operate it while you go off to live the life of your dreams. You may still be the full owner or may have sold down some of your shareholding. Some owners like to stay involved as an executive director or as chairman of the board. You can do whatever you wish – it is still mostly your business. However, the point is that you don't have to be involved in any very active way unless you want to. You will have grown the business to a point where it can afford good managers and it can run very profitably without you.

EXAMPLE

Jim's contracting business started off very small – just Jim and his dad and a lorry. Over the years Jim added staff, including his young son, Sam, more lorries and other heavy machinery. Jim's dad died and Jim was left with the business on his own. Despite some lean years when the building market was slow and there was little investment in infrastructure, Jim survived and was well positioned when the markets recovered and the boom years arrived for contractors. Jim always harboured dreams of a different lifestyle – much different from twelve-hour days, working in all weathers with frequent call-outs over the weekends and holidays to deal with road slips, flood damage and all the rest of it.

Jim has ensured that Sam has been developed well over the years. He received no favours as the boss's son; in fact he has done every job in the business from the bottom up. He has earned the respect of his fellow workers for that and is well on the way to understanding how every aspect of the business is run. Sam, however, is still only twenty-five and in Jim's opinion too young and inexperienced in management to take over. In the meantime Jim has hired an experienced contracting manager (Max) to lead the business while he takes a back seat and Sam develops his management and leadership skills. While there is a significant salary to cover for Max, Jim believes that it is well worthwhile so that he can experience these years of freedom while still in the prime of life. Jim is still involved as chairman and owner, but this requires little of his time.

3. Develop a business that generates big cash flows and suck them out

Many businesses are not saleable at a big price and never will be. Most consulting and advisory businesses fall into this category. You can still become wealthy and free, but it will not be through an eventual sale. These types of businesses are very good at generating high fees and usually have relatively low costs – little infrastructure or fixed costs. The strategy to follow here is to focus on being able to get very good levels of income along the way and to take them out and invest them elsewhere as you go. Generation of significant positive cash flow is paramount!

EXAMPLE

Michelle is a freelance marketing consultant. She honed her skills in the usual way – working for a variety of businesses including spells at an advertising agency and near the top of the marketing department at a nationally recognised consumer goods firm. She now works from a small office where she employs a full-time marketing assistant/PA. She has good associates she can recommend for projects outside her field when that is what her clients need. These associate arrangements are informal: no commissions are paid. Sometimes she receives referrals from these associates too.

Michelle considered building up a marketing consulting business for sale, but realised that, unless she became quite large with lots of staff and created a well-established brand, there would not be anything to sell in the end. After a few false starts and some disappointing experiments partnering with other consultants, she decided to go it alone. She is busy and can command a high hourly rate as she is well known in the industry from previous roles and award-winning work.

Michelle understands that the high fees she gets are prob-ably all the money she will ever receive for her skills. She knows that she needs to use this money well and has engaged an adviser to ensure that she follows a sound investment plan. Her business is a great vehicle for creating cash, but she knows that there will be little of value to sell when she is ready to stop. In the meantime she is focused on building up wealth outside the business. To date she has accumulated a healthy property portfolio and a good spread of shares. She is confident that she will be financially free by forty-five.

Which one will work for you?

If you are not already following a clear strategy to achieve wealth and freedom through your business you should choose whichever of the above strategies best suits your business. In our experience business owners seldom become wealthy by chance: the smart ones have a clear strategy to create the wealth that will eventually set them free.

If your business doesn't deliver on one of the three strategies outlined above you should get out: you are fishing in a dry ditch and your money and energy would be better invested elsewhere. However, before you give up altogether, have a good look at your business – you may well be able to adapt it from its current shape to one that will work for you.

ARE YOU FISHING IN A DRY DITCH?

For you to have a business rather than a job, you need to create wealth through your business that will create some freedom for you.

Killer Question

Can your business create wealth?

Some more hard questions:

- Is your business thriving? Or are you just surviving … or even slipping below the surface?
- Does your business have the potential to follow one of the three strategies for wealth creation?
- Can the business make good money?

If the answer to any of these questions is negative, it's not always your fault. You may have unwittingly entered an industry or a business that will always struggle to make money. It does not pay to fish for business profits in a dry ditch. Have a good hard think about the industry you are in. Is it a profitable industry? Are margins good? Are other people making good money? Is the industry very volatile or cyclical, e.g. farming? If the answers are not to your liking you may want to take your skills, energy and effort somewhere else. Business skills are highly transferable.

Sometimes the problem lies in the part of the industry you operate in. Take the motor industry. Many businesses thrive in the automotive sector e.g. operating good service station franchises, selling new/used cars. But some parts of the sector are squeezed tightly. Repairs and maintenance is a good example. Insurance companies force repair businesses to tender for business, cars are more reliable than ever, qualified staff are hard to find and keep, and the consumer is demanding ever higher standards of service at no extra charge. In addition you have high set-up costs and lots of competition. People shop around and buy on price. This is a very hard business to differentiate yourself in so that you can charge a premium. You may find yourself just working for wages – and barely covering them. If this describes your situation you will want to think about how you can vary your offer so that you are different or better in some way that the customer values. Then you will stand out from the crowd and earn the 'right' to charge a higher price.

The part of an industry that makes money often keeps changing. In the 1980s IBM was the giant in the computer industry. That was when computing was about mainframe computers that took up whole air-conditioned rooms in the businesses that were big enough to afford a computer. Then the personal computer arrived and Hewlett Packard and Digital and Compaq put them in every office and made a bundle for a while. A few years ago people were paying thousands of euros/pounds for a PC that was not as powerful as your mobile phone is today. And it didn't stop there. Now PCs are a commodity – we have classrooms of them. Some homes have two or three and you can get a set-up for less than €500. Now the computer industry is all about software rather than hardware – we pay the big money to Microsoft, Apple, Sony and Sega for programmes, music and games. Pity the person who does not see the changes coming in time. This concept is known as value migration – the place where the money is made (value) shifts in the industry. Have you got stuck in the wrong place? Can you see a shift coming? Do you need to migrate upstream or downstream in your industry?

Some other types of business have a naturally high mortality rate. The restaurant industry is one such. There is so much competition and there are so many things to get right – or wrong! In addition it is a fashion industry – you can be doing just fine and then suddenly the fickle market moves on to the next 'hot' chef, location or cuisine. It is very tempting for people who love to cook or shop or make beautiful things to be lured into thinking that they can make money by opening a gift shop or making and selling craft or serving food. We don't (unfortunately) get much business or financial education at school and therefore often think that something we like (food) or others like (shopping) or that we are good at (making things, fixing things) is a sufficient basis for a business. Those things are necessary, but they are not sufficient to create a good business that can make money on a sustainable basis.

Don't despair – you can adapt!

The message here is that you need to examine your business model carefully. If you are stuck in a poor position that does not have a good future you might as well cut your losses and get out. Alternatively, if this analysis helps you see what is currently wrong with your business you may be able to 'morph' your business into something that has a better chance of creating wealth.

EXAMPLE

Ric had been running his car repair business for several years. Despite being well known in the industry and busy enough to keep several mechanics fully employed, he struggled to do any more than make ends meet. The industry is very competitive and customers shop around for price. The business essentially sells time and that is a difficult model with which to create wealth. In addition margins are low – you have to be able to command high prices if you are to make money by selling time. Anything that goes wrong – absenteeism, illness, rework – blows the budget. Despite being very good at what he does and working very hard, Ric could see that this business model would never deliver wealth and freedom. After some considerable time spent strategising and discussing his model Ric has started to sell reconditioned cars. This is a high margin business and one that sits well alongside his other work. His business already has the tools, space and skills to do the job and he can take advantage of the customer database he already has. Margins have greatly improved and the business is now showing steady profits.

Remember, this is all about the future you want and the life you want to lead. You can't afford to waste your life energies fishing in a dry ditch trying to prove that your original choice was correct. And we have seen lots of business owners do just that. Assume that your business model has problems – almost every business does. Find them. Assess what needs to be done to put you in a better position. Act like your own consultant – you know your industry and your business better than anyone. You want a business that can create wealth and freedom and not just a job. Face the truth. It's your wealth and freedom that's on the line.

First, show me the money!
Try to clarify exactly how money is made in your business.

What do you do? How do you do it? How much money comes in? How much does it cost you to do whatever you do? How much is consumed within the business? Which parts of the business make money and which parts spend money? How much is left at the end – profits?

It can be very useful to draw this out on a sheet of paper or whiteboard. If you have others who can help you or who are knowledgeable about your business it is a very helpful exercise to do as a group.

EXAMPLE

The diagram below shows how this might be for a business providing some form of consultancy like marketing, engineering, surveying, human resource, recruitment or other kinds of advice and expertise.

Business Model for a Consultancy

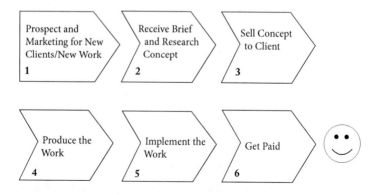

The business has to outlay a lot of time and effort to find clients to whom they can sell. They may have a great deal of skill and expertise but this business is still selling time. Even when they find a prospective client or revisit an established client there is time required for taking a brief and researching the concept. This may or may not be chargeable. Similarly with selling the concept to the client, there may be considerable rework at this point. The business then has to do the work. This may also involve implementing the work in the client's business – working with the client's own people or with external agencies or customers of the client. At this stage the business can bill the client (they may be able to get staged or progress payments from the start if they are lucky or have a well-established relationship with the client) and, hopefully, will be paid in a timely fashion.

The question the business owner has to address here is whether he can charge a high enough rate to cover all of the costs that appear in this model – time that is un-billable, travel, premises, doing work in advance of payment, etc. Many people who are working for someone else see the big gap between what they are paid and what their employer charges out for their time. When they set up in business they often overlook all of the costs that are in the business model and that must be covered out of the fees they charge.

A manufacturing business model will be even more complicated, as there are usually capital costs for plant and equipment, labour costs and distribution costs as well as the marketing and operations costs illustrated above. Considerable amounts of money may be tied up in inventory and work in progress. Some owners' business models fail to take into account how long their cycle is, i.e. how long it takes for raw materials to move through the business, turn them into a completed product, get them sold and get paid. This model may be so long and expensive that it may be next to impossible to get customers to pay the high prices needed to cover it.

So diagram the way that your business works and then ask yourself whether your business can make enough money based on what you think you can charge (or what you can charge if you differentiate yourself to charge higher than you are currently charging) and what you know you will have to spend. You may need to have several attempts at capturing everything on your diagram and getting the numbers that you need.

My Business Model

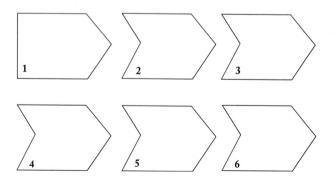

Ask some hard questions about your business model:

- If you were not already in this business would you enter it again?
- Does the wealth-creating recipe of your business look sound?
- Would you buy this business?

These are very challenging questions, but they are not an attempt to make you feel bad about what you are doing. Rather, we are trying to see if you have a job that is just about creating an income for you or a business which has the potential to make you wealthy and free, before you go any further. Many business owners that we see feel a lot of shame because their business is not doing well. When we pull apart their business model it is sometimes clear that no one could make good money in the industry – the model simply does not allow for enough wealth to be created. It is far better to understand where the problem is before you spend a lot more time and money trying to fix or grow a business that may not be fixable in its present form.

Developing a Stronger Business Model

Your business is a wealth-creating asset. Sometimes when you look closely at how the business works it may not have enough potential for creating value. Don't despair. Instead, start to look for ways to get out of having a 'job' and to start having a business – a business better at creating wealth. We have seen many businesses adapt to successfully generate more wealth. These examples will show you a selection of ways you can adapt. You can then decide which one is most appropriate for your business.

Broaden the scope of the business

If your business does something quite specific you may have materials and skills in your business that are transferable to other areas that can expand your customer base and/or increase the range of products or services you offer to your current customers.

EXAMPLE

Jack's printing business was ticking along quite nicely but it wasn't making a lot of money. When we analysed Jack's model it was obvious that the business was a bit of a revolving door:

Jack and his people had to spend a lot of time chasing down orders and often there was no repeat business so the whole sequence had to start all over again. In addition printing is very competitive so it was hard to maintain margins. He was making a living but he had a job not a business and it was hard to see how it would make him wealthy and create freedom. Jack then broadened the scope of his business by adding a design facility. This worked in a number of ways. The designers attracted clients that would never have come to the printing business and so fed the printing side. Work has increased, as when clients experience good design they usually start to review all of their printed materials. In addition, because the designs and plates were still in Jack's business, clients tended to default to him for repeat work. Design is not as price sensitive as printing – it is more creative and more personal and therefore harder to shop for comparisons – so margins are higher. The synergy works in the other direction too: many printing customers are now easily persuaded that they should add a design (or redesign) element to their printing jobs. Jack's business operates from a much more sustainable model now. It makes greater profits and it is a more valuable business for sale.

Focus the business

If your business provides a wide range of products or services to a range of customers you may be able to identify the areas where there is a particularly high demand or better profits to be made, or where you have a particular strength or expertise. It may make sense to put most of your energy into building up this area of your business to the stage where you are the 'go-to' people for anyone seeking that product or service, and to stop wasting your energy on other areas.

EXAMPLE

Mike and Jacinta had a business importing frozen products for distribution to supermarkets, food manufacturers and restaurants. They traded in seafood, vegetables, fruit and occasional consignments of things that seemed like a good buy. They bought all over the world and had long-standing relationships with vendors everywhere these things were produced. Their model was very time-consuming and costly: they had to be knowledgeable of and well known across the markets in several fields, and margins on some of the products were very low. They had a huge amount of stock to store and their warehouse freezers were bulging. While they and their team worked very hard, they were making very little money – just covering wages and their own were small. They had jobs, not a business and it was no recipe for wealth and freedom. It seemed very unlikely that anyone would ever want to buy them out.

After a lot of thought Mike and Jacinta decided to focus on the fruit market. Margins were better and consumer demand was rising. There was increasing demand from restaurants and food manufacturers for top quality fruit products and demand for organic fruit was almost insatiable. Narrowing the product range and focusing the business tightly in one area would allow them to use their expertise to grow their dominance in their area. It would also make better use of their facilities – they would be less likely to be out of stock if they had fewer lines of greater quantity and much of their distribution costs would disappear as they would be serving a narrower number of clients with bigger quantities. The business is much more profitable now – and Mike and Jacinta are paid properly for their efforts. In addition they have built a reputation and a position in their market that should make them an attractive business for sale with some considerable goodwill. They now have a business, not jobs.

Define the offer differently

We have mentioned several times already how it can be difficult to create wealth if you are simply selling time – such a business is limited by the amount of time you can sell and there is seldom a saleable business when you want to stop.

EXAMPLE

Alf found himself in that position as a landscape designer. He was very creative and original but found that no matter how hard he worked (or worked his team) it was difficult to create much value beyond a decent salary. With his skills he could have achieved that anywhere. He understood very quickly that his model needed to change. Over a period of time he has added implementing the designs to his design business – now his people come and do the actual planting and landscaping. Alf can source the shrubs, plants, irrigation systems and garden features at very good prices so can make a significant margin here. He has also developed maintenance contracts with most of his clients so that his people tend plants, mow lawns, monitor irrigation and replace any ailing greenery as needed. Alf has redefined his business from landscape design to worry-free gardens – he takes care of everything from A to Z. This new model is far more profitable and more robust as it is selling much more than time. The on-going contracts he has with hotels and major businesses as well as private homes and small apartments (through designer 'garden walls') create a big barrier for competitors and make his business more valuable and saleable.

'Productise' your service

Service businesses often end up selling only time. One of the solutions is to introduce proprietary products into the mix. Recruitment consultancies can sell psychological testing, trainers sell particular branded training packages, hairdressers can use and up-sell expensive treatment products. It is worth considering if there is any aspect of what you offer that can be turned into a standalone product.

EXAMPLE

Maria's speciality as a human resources consultant was management training. She had a very good name in the industry and was in great demand, but her earnings were clearly limited by the number of days she could present and bill. She developed a range of products that related to her expertise but could be used – and bought – without her. These included skills tests, electronic training modules, management board games and manuals. Her clients are eager to purchase these whenever she presents. They represent added value to the client. For Maria these are a second stream of income and as the range has developed Maria has found further sales outside her client group. She is now providing webinars for offshore clients whom she has never met! This side of the business is very profitable and eminently saleable, whereas it is doubtful if Maria could ever sell her consultancy despite her A-list clients.

Template your business

Many businesses don't work because they are too small or have only one outlet. You may need critical mass to make the model work. For example, one sandwich bar is unlikely to work well enough to make you rich, but a chain of them is a winner! You can spread marketing costs and the development of a brand across many stores. Your purchasing is far more cost effective. Many businesses get stuck at the level of one outlet or remain too small because the owner is carrying the business in his head or has to be involved in every decision or every aspect of the business because the systems have never been documented – or worse, there are no systems at all. It can be very wasteful to run the business like this as it takes very good people to run a business that isn't well organised – if there are no systems, policies, rules or procedures, you need the owner or other high calibre people to make all these decisions. If the business systems are well pinned down and there are good routines almost anyone can run it. Our favourite example is McDonald's – a business with such good systems that it can be run by sixteen-year-olds! Needless to say there are good managers in the background but the point stands – the templates for running the business are in place and it makes it easy to open new outlets and easy to be efficient. A good template of how your business works allows you to get much better efficiencies in the running of your business and allows your senior people to concentrate on improvements rather than just keeping the wheels turning. Your business model may need you to be much bigger or have several outlets in order to give you the scale to make you rich and free. You may need to start by developing systems that will allow the business to scale up.

Does the Business Pay You?

Owners of small businesses often try to fudge the numbers by working for nothing. And they are often doing the job of several people! The model does not work if the business cannot afford to pay you. This may be acceptable for a short period when you are starting out. However, we believe that you should at least give yourself a salary on paper if only to do the numbers properly. And you should set a date at which the business should be paying an actual salary into your account. And if the business cannot meet that, you need to confront the awkward questions and have another look at it all.

Not only does the business need to pay you, but it should be paying you commensurate with your skills, time invested and level of your role. This is a complicated way of saying, 'Pay yourself properly!' For example, if you left a job where you were paid a salary package of €50,000, then you need to be getting close to €50,000 out of your business or you are wasting your time. Every year that you don't earn this money is a year further away from wealth and freedom.

And that's before we ask whether it's paying you enough in salary and drawings to compensate for the effort, risk and investment you have made. You need to get a return on your capital as well as on your labour. You need to examine what you are being paid and whether it is enough. You need to be paid what you are worth. It is not in your interests to fool yourself about this. After all, it is your health, wealth and freedom that are at stake.

Value your time

You need to ask yourself the questions listed below and use the table to estimate what you should be earning from your business in the future.

- What are you worth on the open job market?
- How many hours are you working for your business?
- What are you paid per hour now?
- What should you be paid per hour?
- What targets will you set for the short and medium term?

Income	Today	+ 1 Year	+ 3 Years
Before Tax Per Annum	€	€	€
After Tax Per Annum	€	€	€
Net Per Week	€	€	€
Net Per Hour	€	€	€

Set a target date and make it happen! You need to put the proper value on your time. That will help in focusing your attention on the most important parts of the business. It will also make you think about the hours you work. It will turn your attention to the prices you need to charge and, in turn, how good or how different you will need to be to command those prices. In other words, valuing yourself very highly will prompt all sorts of other questions and decisions that are in the interest of your speedy journey to business success, wealth and freedom.

Valuing your time properly will make you very business-like about your business and your financial freedom.

What's Your Edge?

That may seem like an awkward question. However, there's no point in competing if you have no edge or competitive advantage. This is business – if you are not competitive, then don't compete. So what kind of edge do you have? This could vary from an innovative product, to convenient location, to expertise, to superior service, to speed. Almost anything can give you a competitive edge. What you really don't want to do is be exactly the same as everyone else. If that is the case the only way you can compete is by cutting your prices and that is a fast way to business hell unless you have such huge volumes of business that you make it up in quantity. That is usually not a game that a smaller business can win and is best left to the purchasing and organisational prowess of the huge discounters or the fast food chains.

What are you really good at? Is it something that your market values? Could you be the best at it? You won't necessarily have to be the best in the world or even the best in your class, but you will need to stand out in your area or from your immediate competition. Your service station could be the fastest or friendliest or most conveni-ent or have the best shop or be the most helpful in the general area. Similarly your coffee shop could have the nicest staff, the fastest service or the best children's play-box, or be most friendly to senior citizens. None of these are necessarily original or difficult to organise, but they may make a very big difference to your trade, turnover and profit.

You have to know the one or few things that your business can do extremely well. Then you must stay focused on it/them. Growing your wealth depends on your edge.

Areas in which you might have an edge:

- product quality
- location
- convenience
- service
- customer care
- franchise
- proprietary brands or processes
- after sales service
- expertise
- online presence and information transfer e.g. blogging.

You need to know what you are able to do better or differently than the competition in order to win with your business. The things you choose to have an edge in have to be things that your customers or clients value – it is a great waste of effort and money to build difference in your business that the customer doesn't care about. But just doing the same as everyone else is unlikely to give you the advantage you need to create wealth and freedom through your business.

There's money in muck

People gravitate to glamorous businesses. We have already mentioned the tendency to open restaurants or own small retail shops. The big money gets hooked unwisely into businesses like airlines or car racing. However, if you are prepared to do work that others don't like or won't do, there is often a killing to be made.

Waste management, cleaning and storage are obvious examples. While these types of business often lack glamour and status, the returns are often very high. Is there an opening for your business to refocus in an area that others are ignoring? There is often a lot of money left on the table if you are prepared to do what others will not.

Similarly, we have seen businesses that corner a low margin niche such as cleaning, gardening or waste management that are unlikely to attract too much competition. These versions of flying 'under the radar' of your most obvious competitors can have very valuable payoffs.

It is also worth considering all of the 'extra' streams of revenue that can be attached to your business at very little additional cost to you. You may be able to take most of the additional revenue straight to the bottom line. This extra money can accelerate you along the journey to wealth and freedom. Think about some of the less glamorous additions you could bolt on to your business to add value for the customer and make you some easy money. Examples that we have seen include:

- Electricians and plumbers who remove and dispose of old appliances for a fee, saving you the hassle of a trip to the dump or the recycling station.

- Gardeners who remove branches, grass and other waste at a charge and who then recycle it as compost – for which they also charge.

- Automotive workshops that also sell car accessories and gifts for car lovers – they have already paid for the premises and staff and are doing this as a convenience for customers, not as an attempt to challenge the big accessory retailers.

- Online games for kids that send weekly activity reports and options for upgrades to parents.

- Carpet cleaners who have added furniture cleaning and protection from stains and carpet mites to their repertoire – they have already made the trip to your house.

- Recruitment consultants who will write up contracts of employment, job descriptions and offers of employment – all saving you the hassle and earning them an additional fee.

Money – and profit – is no respecter of glamour. Often there is a lot of value left on the table in your business. Look around at what you do and consider the needs of your clients and customers – are there products or services you could offer them that might easily bring additional income at little cost to you?

Failing to Plan is Planning to Fail

Planning is all about deciding in advance what needs to be done. Peter Drucker, one of the best thinkers about business, wrote: 'Whenever you see a successful business, someone once made a courageous decision.' That's essentially what strategy and planning are for – making decisions and making them in advance rather than just on the hoof. We all have to make many small decisions as we go, but the bigger ones – about new products and services, about which segments of the market we will serve, about investment – need to be made carefully and well in advance.

Plans don't need to be complicated or long. It is the time and effort spent thinking and talking about the business and the future that makes all the difference. Do you know where your business is headed? Have you decided what the most important issues to address are? Do you know which aspects of the business you should reinvest in?

A plan is a map for your business – it should show the destination you want to reach, it should have the main routes marked and some of the big features you need to navigate around. Everyone in the business needs to be working off the same map. A prime purpose of creating the map is to inform those drawing up the plan. A map allows you to have 'one version of the truth' in your business – here's the territory, here's where we're going, here's what we have to gear up for on the way, here are the milestones.

Planning 'prayer' to be chanted at least once a day!

Proper

Prior

Planning

Prevents

Poor

Performance

The Planning Process

Flow chart of the Planning Process

| **Where do we want to be?** |
| The dream or vision for the business: where you want to get to, e.g. a business that can be sold in five years. |

↓

Where are we today?
Opportunities and threats, current strengths and weaknesses, the competition we face, our customers' demands, our resources, etc.

↓

What are the big things we need to do?
Picking the key areas where you have to get results – the market you are going to serve (or exit), the products and services you are going to provide (or not), the staff you need to hire (or have and should not), the skills you need to build – you are choosing how you will win!

↓

How will we do them?
Putting together a brief plan to make it happen.

↓

How will we track our progress?
Our measurement scorecard, our milestones, our key indicators of performance, our dashboard.

While the process described in the flow chart above looks logical and linear, you need to keep revising each stage as you consider new things, e.g. you might develop a dream and then move on to looking at this business as it is now. That will send you back to modify the dream. The process of planning is iterative – you have to keep going through the steps – planning is always a work in progress. It is never over!

Who in your business should plan?

Everybody who works in the business should be involved in some way. Obviously, you the business owner must take overall responsibility for the planning and the decisions. However, your people will know some things about your business and your customers that you don't! It is wasteful not to harness everyone's energy and ideas and your business cannot afford that waste.

People also support what they help to create. If you want your people to implement decisions well, then they need to understand how and why they were made. People feel respected and responsible when they are included – even if they don't seem to contribute very much to the planning. You may not need or want to involve everyone in every planning session, but they should all be involved in some aspect of it. You can also put it down to training and development – everyone learns a lot more about the business and how it works. This informs the decisions they are making every day anyway – and often without you around. The better they all understand the business and the consequences of what they do, the better they perform.

Killer Question

Why does your business exist?

Many business owners are unclear about the business they are in, why it exists. You may well be a very good plumber ... are you in the business of plumbing new homes? Of solving domestic crises? Of rescuing frantic mothers from blocked drains and overflowing washing machines? Of being available when no one else is?

You may have an accountancy practice. Are you in the business of doing annual accounts? Of minimising tax? Of providing business advice? Of being a trusted adviser?

These are all very different businesses that require different marketing, different staffing, different levels of customer service, different operational skills. If you don't know what business you are in it is very difficult to get anything else right – you will tend to be all over the place, trying to do everything but not doing anything particularly well.

You should never stop asking this question. It helps you to decide what you need to start doing and, just as important, what you should stop doing. If you know what business you are in it is very clear what businesses you are not in!

A PEEST of a future

It is very easy to overlook the fact that tomorrow will be different. Many businesses get blind sided by changes that, in hindsight, were fairly obvious. Every business needs to keep an eye on the future – looking for changes that might impact on your business. 'Futuring' is not an exact science, but it will keep you alert to change – and every little bit of additional time to plan for changes you foresee is invaluable.

A convenient format for scanning the future is to use the acronym PEEST:

- **Political** (government, regulations, legal, tax)
- **Economic** (inflation, recession, interest rates, foreign exchange, wages)
- **Environmental** (legislation, lobby groups, sustainability movement)
- **Social** (culture, lifestyles, opinions, demographics)
- **Technological** (internet, e-business, medical, communications, speed, ease, cost)

PEEST analysis is best done by having participants consider individually what issues the organisation may face in the future under the above headings. Sharing these observations usually leads to further ideas and the group can then prioritise the issues in terms of the opportunities or threats presented to the business.

EXERCISE:

List trends or issues that may affect your business under each of the PEEST headings. Decide whether you think the trend or issue is a threat or an opportunity. For example, you might identify a trend for people to work from home:

- **Opportunity** – can your business provide them with something they will want at home?

- **Threat** – they may not use what you currently produce at home.

Big rocks – strategic issues that have to be tackled

As you plan, you will want to capture a list of the big items that you need to address. This will help you isolate the things that will make the most difference. It can be very difficult in a business to focus on the strategic issues – the really important stuff – when there are so many urgent (but often minor) issues screaming for your attention. One of the payoffs of planning is that you become clear about what should be on the list of stuff that really matters. You will keep amending this list and the priorities will keep changing as you plan. That's why you have to think and plan all year, not just once a year. Use your PEEST results to begin a list of big issues to tackle. It's important to compile a list of trends or projections that the business will face over the next five years and the most important strategic issues that need to be addressed as a result.

EXAMPLE

Trend: Customers are demanding increasing levels of service and are very impatient … and short of time.

Issue: Speed – we need to achieve same day turnaround for our service (currently three to four days).

When you do some work on analysing your opportunities for growth, your competitors, your customers and so on, you will want to come back to this list and continue to refine it.

SWOT your planning

SWOT (strengths, weaknesses, opportunities, threats) analysis is a handy way of looking both at what is likely to happen in the future and how well your business is positioned to deal with the future. It works best if you consider opportunities and threats first (after all, the strengths and weaknesses of your business are relative to the opportunities and threats that you face). Traditionally, organisations have conducted SWOT beginning with an internal analysis. It may be smarter to consider opportunities and threats first and then consider the organisation in the light of its ability to respond to the external situation. This may be particularly important for organisations that are mature and inclined to be inwardly or historically focused. Whichever sequence you choose, the process works best if it is iterative (go backwards and forwards through it several times).

Use the opportunities and threats that you have identified through PEEST. Some things are both an opportunity and a threat. Opportunities and threats are usually outside your organisation. Decide what actions you will need to take in response to them and record your results on a table like this:

Opportunities (to exploit)	Action to be taken
1	
2	
3	
4	
5	
Threats (to reduce/mitigate)	Action to be taken
1	
2	
3	
4	
5	

And then strengths and weaknesses. Strengths and weaknesses are internal to your organisation. You should confine yourself to the ones that are relevant to the opportunities and threats you have identified.

Strengths (to build on)	Action
1 e.g. our very long-serving employees	Retain them
2	
3	

4	
5	
Weaknesses (to eliminate/cope with)	**Action**
1 e.g. too few new employees …	
2	
3	
4	
5	

Planning for growth

Businesses need to grow – if you are not going forwards you are probably going backwards! Businesses never stand still for long – stagnation is just the first step on the way to failure. So what strategies do you need to adopt to ensure that your business grows successfully?

When organisations struggle to grow it is tempting to flail all around looking for new business. A growth matrix allows people to examine the options in a structured way and ensures that key areas are not overlooked.

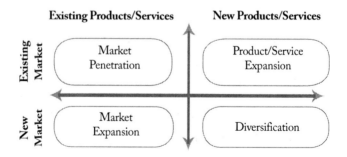

- Start by compiling a list of present products/services. How could you sell more of the same to your existing clients? Unless you have reached saturation/ have overwhelming dominance, market penetration is usually the easiest strategy and often reveals some very 'low-hanging' fruit. Businesses often fail to exploit low-risk strategies before embarking on high-risk ones.

- Then look at how these products/services can be marketed to new markets. Market expansion allows you to take the things you are already good at and to find new users.

- In turn, consider what new products/services could be marketed to existing (happy, loyal) clients and customers whom your people should know and understand the needs of very well. Product/service expansion allows you to leverage your customer knowledge to find new ways of delighting people with whom you already have very sound relationships. They will be more willing to try new offerings from you than customers with whom you have no previous track record.

- Lastly (and this is where people often start!), consider what new offerings could be made to new markets. This is high-risk territory where everything that can go wrong will. Ideas that end up in this diversification quadrant need to be rigorously tested – it is the same as starting a new business!

Pitfalls for planners

Make sure you don't fall into any of these traps:

- **Only 'planning' once a year and then putting it on a shelf to collect dust** – you need to be planning all the time.

- **Starting with where you are rather than where you want to be** – the dream's the thing.

- **Aiming too low** – you'll never get anything moving.

- **Doing a plan** – but then continuing 'business as usual' on Monday and never taking action on the plan.

- **Failing to make tough decisions about what needs to change** – avoiding pain.

- **Going 'offsite' for two days and believing that that's planning** – it's just recreation! Planning is on-going and it's hard work (but fun!).

- **Not having a scoreboard of what's important to measure** (rather than what's easy to measure).

- **Putting all the effort into an impressive written plan rather than into the thinking and the doing.**

- **Using lots of jargon that no one understands.**

Pulling the Plan Together

There are many techniques that you can use to help you think about your business and the strategies that you could pursue and we detail several of them in this section. The more tools you use and the more often you use them the better the thinking and the plan will be.

One page planning

It is really worthwhile keeping your documentation short and simple. A one-page plan is easy to carry around – you'll find that you memorise it anyway.

A useful outline is to think in terms of:

- **Overall Objective** – What are you setting out to do? This often takes a bit of time to clarify. Increase operating profits to prepare for sale of the business? Grow owners' net worth? Capture increased market share? Develop a new division? Expand overseas? You need to be as specific as you can here because the rest of the plan should be geared to achieving this objective.

- **Goals or Key Numbers** – What are the key numbers you need to achieve to realise your objective? These goal areas will vary by business: Revenue? Market share? New products brought to market? Staff numbers? Margins? Net worth? Number of lost hours? The numbers/goals you use here should make a real difference to the business – otherwise why are they here?

- **Key Issue or Strategies** – What has to be done (at a relatively high level – these are not little actions)? These are the 'must dos' to achieve your objective: Develop a new product? Close down a division? Outsource an operation? Grow a new organisational capability, e.g. 'Speed' for twenty-four-hour turnaround? Increase average sale to €20? These are the big initiatives that will make a difference to your business.

- **Measures and Milestones** – How you keep score and track your progress and that of others. Think in terms of quantity, quality and time – How much? How well? By when? If you don't get clear about tracking your progress you will stay 'trying' to make these things happen rather than actually 'doing' them and measuring your progress frequently.

- **Specific Actions** – What are the main activities that need to take place?

It is harder to fill in one page with good stuff than ten pages with padding and drivel. But working to a single page plan will make you think all the harder – and it's a great discipline for your team. They can do one-page plans for each of their areas of responsibility.

Try it – it really works!

EXAMPLE

Jane Smith has a retail clothing shop in the centre of a mid-size town. While not attempting to compete with the large chains, there is nevertheless a market for convenient locally available clothes of good quality. The area is quite wealthy and the market not particularly price driven. Many of the residents are older and want to shop locally. Jane is confident that as long as the quality is sustained the shop has a good future.

Jane has done a great deal of thinking about the business. While she enjoys her work and lifestyle she wishes to retire from retail in the medium-term future and wants to be able to sell the business for a good price – after all that is why she went into business and took those risks in the first place!

Here's how she came up with her one-page plan using the structure described above:

Objective:

After much thought Jane has decided that she wishes to be able to 'retire' five years from now. To fulfil her other dreams she wants to be able to sell the business for €400,000. It is definitely not worth that now – she would be lucky to get €100,000 for it if she could sell it at all. But Jane has decided that she will do what it takes to build the business so that it is worth her asking price.

Goals:

Jane knows that businesses sell on a multiple of earnings – her accountant says that she should look for three to five times her annual profits. To be on the safe side Jane is going to expect about three times earnings. That means she will need profits of about €135,000 if she wants to sell for €400,000. She has set her profit goals – the numbers she has to achieve – accordingly. She has also set revenue goals and gross margin goals as she will need to grow her sales and also increase her margins to achieve those profit figures. (Jane's accountant is helping her work out a detailed budget to support her one-page plan.)

Strategies:

Jane spent a lot of time working out what she could do to build the business to achieve these numbers. She has settled on a combination of strategies for the first year to grow sales, reduce costs and sell more at greater margin. Jane will continue to refine these strategies as she considers alternatives.

Some will be harder to achieve than others. Her measures will give her an early indication of whether these strategies are sufficient to meet year one's goals.

Measures:

Jane had to push herself hard to come up with measures for each strategy that were not 'waffling'! She knew she needed to pin herself down if she was to achieve her goals. She found setting numerical measures of quantity, quality and dates hard work, but it made her feel very realistic about the challenges she was setting herself.

Actions:

Jane used the one-page plan to note some of the things she needed to get started or delegate as she planned. It gave her a place to begin accomplishing her dream!

OBJECTIVE: Build the business to sell for €400,000			
GOALS	Year 1	Year 3	Year 5
1. Revenue	€960,000	€1,210,000	€1,350,000
2. Net profit	€80,000	€110,000	€150,000
3. Gross margin	37%	39%	41%

STRATEGIES	MEASURES	ACTION PLANS
1. Improve Purchasing	• Initiate stocktake • Take marketing advice on lines • Analyse last three years' sales by line items	• Find new supplier of linens
2. Avail of all discounts on offer	• Take prompt payment discount each month	• Investigate discounts for bulk purchase of low risk items, e.g. sweatshirts
3. Only two sales each year	• Sale in July school holidays • Sale on 26 December	• Promote heavily through local and social media • Consider discount coupon offer – joint venture?

4. Drive full margin sales through preview events	• Sell 30% of new season stock at full margin	• Develop database of higher spenders (use credit card purchases) • Delegate to Mary Ann • Wine and cheese event?
5. Grow sales through development of own brand label	• Initial product lines by March year one • Gross margin of 40% • Target as 20% of sales total	• Seek additional manufacturing partner
6. Control discounts	• By end of month	• Written policy revoking staff discretion to offer discounts
7. Increase store traffic	• Increase traffic by 5% each year	• Install people counter • Investigate loyalty card

Knowing what not to do!

Michael Porter, the renowned business strategist, said that the essence of strategy is knowing what not to do. You often can't focus on what you should do until you make clear decisions about what not to do – what not to get into in the first place or to get out of if you are already in! Consider the business lines you should get out of, the activities you should outsource, the areas of the country you should no longer operate in, the segments of the market you should stop trying to serve …

Deciding what not to do is critical! You may find your SWOT analysis useful for this. If you have identified a particular area as a weakness in your business, or as under threat, this may be the area that you should avoid.

BUILD YOUR OWN DASHBOARD

Key performance indicators in your business

One of the most difficult aspects of running a business is that there is so much happening, so much going on at any particular time, that it is very difficult to know what to give attention to. Many owners and managers solve this by being manic – chasing around, putting out fires, flitting from issue to issue. They do this at great cost to themselves. It's a horrible way to manage – and to live. They pay a big price in terms of time, stress and health. And, to add insult to injury, it's very bad for the business.

Killer Questions

If you were stranded on a desert island for a year and could only receive scraps of information by carrier pigeon occasionally, what three measures of performance in your business would you most want to monitor?

What really matters in your business?

How do you know?

How do you monitor what matters?

What's a dashboard?

Imagine the pilot of a Boeing 747. Just think for a minute about the complicated machine he is piloting. Consider the amount of real-time data and information that he must be aware of at any moment to ensure the safety of the aircraft. And we wouldn't want him to get out on the wing mid-flight to measure ice build-up, or check how much fuel is left, or have a 'recce' on the weather!

Solution: Decades of flight have resulted in aircraft designers and engineers choosing a range of instruments to monitor and measure the critical functions of the aircraft. It will be a bit more complicated than a car, with which we are all familiar, but no doubt speed, altitude, fuel, global positioning, etc., figure large. The pilot is freed to monitor the key dials rather than having to collect data and choose what information he will attend to at any moment. He can pilot the plane while keeping an eye on the key dials. He will take corrective action if any of the gauges indicate that the plane is outside a recommended range of measures. Just as in our cars, the dials will probably have red zones or flashing lights or even alarms to assist the pilot to recognise that he is outside the appropriate zone.

Similarly, in business no human could pay attention to all of the details that might be important. It would be very difficult to decide which ones were critical if all of the information was lumped together. By deciding what the critical indicators on the dashboard should be, the task is made manageable.

The challenge for every business is to develop a dashboard of indicators that works to manage and ensure the success of that business.

Why your business needs a dashboard

- **Focus** – so that you concentrate your efforts on what matters.

- **Clarity** – so that everyone knows what's important around here.

- **Accountability** – so that people know what they are responsible for – and so that they know that you know how they are doing on the key measures.

- **Communication** – so that you can talk about the right stuff in terms that everyone understands.

- **Consistency** – so that every month you focus on the same key things rather than on whatever grabs the attention of the moment.

- **Management** – so that you can easily see what needs to be worked on and whether the actions you are taking are having the desired effect.

The few things that matter (remember Pareto!)

In every business (and, indeed, every area of life) there are a few things that really matter and many, many other things that don't. The small number of things that matter are critical levers in the business. By definition, they are 'make or break' issues. Obvious areas spring to mind like sales, margins, operating profit. When you don't hit the right numbers in these areas you go out of business – fast!

But it can be a lot more difficult to figure out what drives sales or profits – i.e. what are the key drivers in your industry and your particular business. Sales, for example, could be driven by advertising, price, location, range, quality, reputation, weather – or a combination of these, depending on the business.

It is very difficult to manage your business – or to know what deserves your attention – if you are not clear about what is critical to your business.

The things which matter most must never be at the mercy of the things which matter least.

Goethe

You can't manage what you can't measure

Many businesses measure very little. Not a good idea, as by the time you know you have a problem it may be too late. Others have a range of indicators to measure things such as customer service or net profit levels. Some have been chosen because everyone uses them or the accountant said so! Others may be chosen because they are easy to measure. None of these approaches is ideal – each business needs to do some work on deciding what is important for that particular business to measure.

Finding what key indicators to measure

There is a logical sequence to working out what measurement indicators matter in your business – and it should follow your strategic planning process:

1. **Mission – Do you know what your business exists to do?** What product/service are you providing to whom? (e.g. general printing services to small business and the public, legal services to local geographical area, fat lambs to the premium export market, Italian food to a discerning clientele.) For example, Aer Lingus exists to fly people (rather than planes) domestically and internationally. My business exists to _____

2. **Key results areas (KRAs) – What areas do you have to get results in?** What are the key deliverables in your business? What achievements must you produce for the business to be successful? Which areas of the business have to function really well in what ways in order for your business to succeed? (e.g. a printing business would focus on efficient production and sales, a law firm on providing advice and securing clients, a farmer on growing grass and converting it into meat, a restaurant on food and service.) Think marketing, production, sales, purchasing, inventory, distribution and service, and ask what the key deliverables are for your business in each area. For example, Aer Lingus has to get more people to fly more often, profitably. My business has to _____

3. **Critical success factors (CSFs) – What factors are critical to your success?** What is it that drives your business? What do your stakeholders really

care about? What is it that you can tweak to make a difference? These will vary business by business, even in the same industry. For example, the printer's customers may value speed, just-in-time delivery and/or a one-stop-shop, the legal clients may value comprehensive services, convenience and local specialisation. Think timeliness, quality, speed, convenience, price, reputation, brand, recruitment, retention, innovation, new products and market share, and ask what you have to do in order to win in your marketplace. For example, Aer Lingus must get costs down so it can offer lower prices and raise margins. My business must _____

4. **Key performance indicators (KPIs) – What are the performance indicators that would provide a good measure for each factor?** How can you measure the factors that you have identified as critical? For example, if speed is an issue you might decide to measure order to fulfilment (days), if productivity is a key factor you might measure billable hours per person or pages printed per hour, if service is a key factor you might measure complaints or measure satisfaction through surveys or repeat business rates. Therefore, Aer Lingus will probably measure forward bookings, online sales, self-check-in by kiosk rates (cheaper and assists higher volume), loadings (efficiency) and customer satisfaction (is it working?). My business will measure:

1 _____

2 _____

3 _____

A balanced dashboard

Your business needs a dashboard of measures that is balanced:

- External and internal stakeholder measures.
- Hard (quantitative, e.g. sales) and soft (qualitative, e.g. satisfaction) measures.
- Financial and non-financial measures.
- Leading (about the future) and lagging (about what's happened) measures.

External and internal stakeholder measures

Who are the key stakeholders in your business? Think owners, customers, staff and suppliers. What's important to them? How do you know? Do you ask? How well does your business rate on each factor that is important to your stakeholders? What are the things you have to get right so that customers, suppliers, shareholders and employees are happy and will allow your business to succeed?

EXERCISE:

Employees usually care very much that they are treated with respect, paid competitively, get lots of feedback and have the opportunity to learn and improve their future prospects:

- What's 'on top' for your staff?

- How well do you rate on the key items that matter to them?

Tip: Employees are usually the least considered group when it comes to business performance measures! Don't let it happen to yours.

Hard and soft measures

Not everything that counts can be counted and not everything that can be counted counts.

Albert Einstein

The quote is partly tongue-in-cheek. However, it does draw attention to the fact that we are all inclined to measure what is easy to measure and often overlook things that are harder to assess.

Consider staff, for example. Employees are critical to the success of most businesses, but it is much easier to count them (and capture demographic and remuneration measures) than to work out how to measure how happy or committed they are. And yet these may be very important to your business, especially if it is difficult to get the kind of staff you want, if it is expensive to train them in your business or if it is important that you keep them for a long time.

Financial and non-financial measures

It is most common to use financial measures. These are often shown as percentages or ratios. Examples include gross profit percentage (profitability), average collections period (efficiency), turnover of cash (liquidity) or interest cover (leverage). But it is also important to monitor aspects of performance that are not financial. Consider days of training, staff morale, feedback, number of good ideas, reputation, response to recruitment, quality of new hires, etc. Non-financial measures are often far more indicative of the future and long-term health of your business. They can also serve as an early-warning system allowing you to identify problems before they hit the bottom line.

Leading and lagging indicators

One of the problems with traditional methods of measuring financial progress is that they are often historical – they tell you what happened last month or last year. It is important to engage with the future rather than just the past or present. Measures of sales or profits usually 'lag' the event itself – good measures, but often arriving too late to help you change your practice quickly enough.

Every business needs some leading indicators as well – measures that are good indicators of what is coming down the line. If you choose good leading indicators your dashboard should give you advance warning that will allow you to adjust in time. Smart business owners know that it is not the health of the business yesterday or today that is really of concern, but rather what things are looking like for the future.

Leading indicators you could consider include: forward bookings, levels of learning, interest rates, suggestions implemented, patent applications, exchange rates, building permits, applications for consents and weather forecasts. Ask yourself what trends matter to your business.

How many measures?

It does not matter how many different measures your business uses. Some businesses will measure hundreds. However, what does matter is that no one should be expected to pay attention to more than a few. So, the trick is to decide what is *vital* – for each area of the business or for each manager. These are the indicators you should always ask about, expect staff to be prepared to talk about and what you should hold people accountable for.

The one measure you absolutely need

A measure of customer satisfaction – or you may have no business!

Examine it as often as possible. Sometimes several measures can be added together to give you an index of satisfaction, e.g. returns, complaints and service failures, and you can give different weight to different measures in your index.

It's part of planning

Obviously there's a strong link to your strategic planning. The measures that end up on your dashboard should be ones that are critical to your business. It is your planning that helps determine what the key areas are that you must get results in and what factors are critical to your success in each area. Your research should tell you how you rate on these factors. Then you must choose measures that allow you to monitor and measure how you continue to perform.

PRODUCTIVITY

Getting more done

Productivity – getting the best outputs from your inputs – is the great challenge for business. In these times of greater global competition, low-priced imports and rising compliance costs, a business must become very focused on producing more or better with less in order to remain competitive and profitable.

Just about every decision an owner or manager makes affects productivity – recruitment, selection, training, promotion, reward – but the decisions are rarely scrutinised in terms of how they will impact on productivity.

There are no quick fixes or magic bullets for achieving greater productivity, but there are a number of ideas that are worth examining to see if you can use them to lift productivity.

Killer Question

Are you getting the best output from your input?

Timelines

Managing the time – and timelines – of the business

effectively is key. Your most profitable customers are often those who are in a hurry or who can't or won't wait for whatever it is they want. They are usually prepared to pay more for quality delivered in a time frame that suits them (if not you). People are busy. Can you get your response time right in order to charge premium prices and achieve higher returns? The best customers are usually the most demanding. Can you get someone there today? Can you quote on the spot or before close of business today? Can the clothing be altered now? Can you reduce manufacturing time or service processing time?

Changing the time frames – being more responsive – often requires no more capital or staff, but instead a change of process. We often get trapped into processes that consume time (or are 'comfortable' for us) and leave a big gap between what we offer and what the customer wants – and is prepared to pay for.

What would you have to do to make the response time faster? What would be the effect on your profitability? For example, many cafés are extremely slow at producing the cup of coffee you order. You have already consumed the muffin or lunch sandwich and are looking anxiously at your watch and wondering if you'll be late for the next meeting. Not only does this tardiness often mean that you choose to forego a break (and a very profitable one for the café), but it also means the opportunity to sell a second cup of coffee is lost in many instances. It is hard to understand why cafés have only one coffee machine for twenty or more tables and why the process seems so amateurish and slow. They will all have their reasons, but the bottom line is that productivity and profitability are adversely affected.

You can charge more for:

- dry cleaning done today
- on demand visits to doctor or dentist
- travel booked at the last moment
- a room for tonight
- out of hours services
- emergency repairs.

EXERCISE

What timeliness or responsiveness could your business charge a premium for?

You can play this idea out in several ways: the shorter the time between the decision to purchase and the actual purchase, the more customers are prepared to pay. Don't hold them up! Don't make them feel that they would be better to shop around! Meet their desires and demands NOW. And make them pay for it.

Re-engineer

Re-engineering as a concept got a bad name when it

became synonymous with making redundancies. The basic concept is very useful, however. The idea is to radically redesign the business processes in order to achieve major gains in cost, service or time.

There are three basic steps:

1. Breaking up the organisation's activities into component parts (mapping out the process).

2. Identifying the inefficiencies.

3. Redesigning the process from scratch.

The fundamental question all the way through is whether the customers would pay for each step in your process if they knew about it – the delays, the double handling, the rework.

EXERCISE

Map out the processes in your business. Use a diagram to show what happens at each stage until the product or service is ready for the customer.

Ask:

- Where do you lose time?
- Why do you do each step in the order that you do?
- Where do errors happen?
- What could be eliminated?

- What aspects of the process could be done at the same time (in parallel)?

What you provide often depends on combining many tasks, stages and people. It is worth sitting around a whiteboard with all concerned and working out where time and effort could be shaved from the process. When you take time and effort out you often take a lot of cost out as well, despite the fact that cost wasn't the original focus. Doing things faster usually means doing them smarter – and it's usually cheaper. For example, self-check-in at the airport was introduced to reduce queues – but it's also much cheaper as well as more convenient, as it only requires a computer rather than a desk attendant.

Do a walk-through

It may take several days or even weeks for an order or even for a request for a quote to pass through your business. You can do an interesting exercise by 'walking' the order through the business, asking each person to act on it right away instead of placing it in an in-tray or a work-in-progress queue. Often the chain takes very little time this way.

You may be surprised at what else may emerge during this exercise. For example, it often becomes clear that the business has fallen into the trap of continuing to do things that need not be done at all or that most of the time taken to produce the product or service is consumed by wait/queuing times. For example, a piece of paper may have to wait many days in several in-trays but only take a short amount of time to deal with each time it reaches the top of the tray. Alternatively, it may be easier to train people to do all or most of the process needed on each job rather than having so many handovers. At the very least, this exercise often identifies bottlenecks that can be addressed by extra resources (machines, operators, skills).

Using capacity

If you have expensive plant and equipment (or buildings or people) then the amount of time you manage to use them for is critical to your productivity. Taxis need to be driven, planes need to spend as little time on the ground as possible, the printing presses need to be running, the shop needs to be open and making sales ... The idea here is that you drive up your productivity by utilising the capacity you have. Likewise if you have staff sitting idle because there is no work available or they are waiting for others to finish something, you have lots of productivity gains to make by reallocating staff or changing the process.

You need to work out how much of your resource is effectively used, such as how many hours (out of a potential twenty-four) your limousines are at work carrying paying passengers. Then you need to examine the factors that contribute to effective use and make the changes needed. In the example here, analysis might show that the booking system is the most important component to affect how productive each limousine can be, and prompt the following questions:

- Have we enough call operators?

- Are they well trained?

- Do they get the client details correct?

- Are they dispatching cars in the best way?

Most problems can be split up in this kind of way. Your business will be most productive if you focus on the factors that account for the greatest loss of productivity.

What stops us?

Sometimes it's easier to problem solve from the other end. You could ask questions like:

- Why can't we do it faster?

- Why can't we make it cheaper (and sell much more/ more often)?

- Why can't we charge a higher price for our goods/ services?

- Why aren't we rated higher for our quality?

- What stops us from achieving these desirable outcomes?

- How real are these blockages?

- Can we shift anything?

- What would it be worth to us to make the changes needed?

Decision-making

The total time taken to make decisions and act may be a key factor in productivity. Consider:

- the time elapsed between noticing a performance problem and doing anything about the person involved (training, managing better, replacing).

- the time lost between needing a new hire and having them begin work.

- the time elapsed from an item appearing on a meeting agenda to a final decision being taken.

If something needs to be addressed, make a decision and do it. Procrastination most often attaches to things we prefer not to do, e.g. tackling a difficult person or dealing with non-performance. However, the pain does not lessen by ignoring the problem. Far from it: the problem usually gets worse, business is lost and productivity suffers. In the interest of productivity Just Do It – NOW! Track a few of your decision-making processes and see where the time is lost – in avoiding issues, in picking them up and putting down, in failing to take action, in revisiting the same issues and arguments over and over. Typically the bigger the business the worse is the efficiency of decision-making. Slow decisions are not better decisions; they are slower decisions (and actions). See if you can speed up the decision-making processes in your business – you might 'decide to decide' on every agenda item, have 'standing up' meetings to introduce a little urgency (discomfort) or put a time limit on issues ('We'll decide by Friday').

Setting priorities

The most important things must be first. There simply isn't time to do everything. And hopping from one issue to the next is never good for productivity. Probably the very best thing an owner can do for the profitability and productivity of the business is to identify the few matters that have priority and show by example a relentless focus on these.

Ask yourself what the few critical results we need in the coming months are (e.g. new premises, reduced raw goods costs, reduced inventory, shorter cycles, greater skill level, new product delivery, customer service, quality). You cannot deliver on all fronts at the same time. It is critical that you identify the few that will be your focus and take whatever actions are necessary to deliver the desired results in those areas. What's the most important or the most urgent? Give yourself and everyone else a clear focus.

Most of the things that will make the difference to your business productivity are highly important but have low urgency – planning, developing new products or services, improving resource utilisation, developing people.

EXERCISE

Use the idea of priority management to audit how you are spending your time (and the time of the business). Fill in the diagram below for a typical week – look in your diary and see how and where you have spent your time. How much time is allocated in each quadrant?

The low urgent/high importance quadrant is typically the most neglected:

Urgency	Urgent but not important (high urgent/low importance)	Urgent and important (high urgent/high importance)
	Not urgent or important (low urgent/low importance)	Not urgent but important (low urgent/high importance)

Importance

People

Productive and responsive people know what is expected of them, have the necessary skills and resources to deliver and will give customers what they want when they want it.

As most business requires a team effort to deliver, this applies to groups as well as individuals.

EXERCISE

Can you say 'yes' to:

- My people know what is expected of them.
- They have the skills to do what is needed.
- They have the resources – materials, time, information – to do the job.
- They have the right attitude and habits to deliver (we have not robbed them of their motivation).

Training your people

Training – appropriate, well chosen, well delivered, properly measured – is essential to productivity. You either need to hire the best people who are already well trained or you need to grow your own.

Check:

- Can they manage their own time and effort or do they require constant (expensive) supervision?

- Can they work to deadlines – and manage priorities?

- Can they problem solve?

- Can they communicate well with each other and the clients?

- Can they compile the needed reports?

- Can they read the reports they are expected to use?

None of these require training to degree level, but the absence of these skills and competencies slows your business down, affects customer satisfaction and lowers your productivity. Estimates vary, but many studies suggest that training is many times cheaper than the cost of being untrained. Think about this in terms of better managing the talent (resources) you already have.

Tools

It is often said that a workman is only as good as his tools. Give your people what they need to do the job as well and as quickly as possible:

- Are there enough tools (e.g. coffee machines)? We have seen people move around a huge warehouse just to access box cutters – there were not enough of them.

- Are the tools good enough – is the software up to the job? Can you get internet access fast enough? Are there enough phone lines for your busy period?

- Is there space and light and heat appropriate to the work? Some working conditions mean that staff are fighting 'hygiene' factors all of the time just to do their job – trying to get the air conditioning to work properly, trying to get in/out of the building (security), trying to park, etc., all before they can turn their attention to getting anything productive done.

Solving these problems won't necessarily make them more productive – but not solving them surely lowers productivity.

FAMILY BUSINESSES

Over half of all the people who are employed in the private sector are working in family owned businesses. Family owned and operated businesses range from small retail shops, service businesses and professional firms to larger construction companies, franchisers and corporations. Almost all farms are family businesses. And family businesses are different!

What is a family business?
A family business is one in which two or more people from the same family work, that is owned by at least one of them. It can be any combination of husband and wife, father, son and daughter, brothers and sisters, dad and his cousins and so on. Any time family members work together they face an interesting range of challenges.

Killer Question

Are you a FAMILY business or a family BUSINESS?

In other words, have you a business that happens to be owned by a family or a family who happens to own a business? The difference is critical. In some family businesses the emphasis is all on the family to the detriment of the business; in others, there is a greater understanding of the needs of the business and the roles that family need to balance.

Here are some more challenging questions:

- What are your priorities?

- Which title do you want more:

    ◊ 'Excellent businessperson' or

    ◊ 'Parent of the year'

- How important is your family? Work?

- What kind of relationship do you want with:

    ◊ Your spouse?

    ◊ Your children?

    ◊ Your employees?

- What are:

    ◊ Your long-term goals?

    ◊ Your spouse's?

    ◊ Your children's?

- Do work and family values conflict? How can you make them complement?

- Have you given any thought to retirement? What would you like to do?

What's the family business for?

The purpose of a business is to create wealth. Even if the family has been in farming or acted as real estate agents for four generations, the business should still be making healthy profits. Does everyone in your family/business understand this or do some of them believe that the business exists to offer them employment, lifestyle or other benefits that they could not command for the same level of effort or skill elsewhere?

Family lore

'The first generation tends it, the second extends it and the third spends it.' Most family companies don't last beyond the founder; very few make it to the fourth or fifth generation.

The main thing that hurts a family business is the family! In a normal business people who are not up to the job can be removed – but if you think firing an employee is hard, try getting rid of your mother's favourite child!

Competitive advantages

There are lots of good reasons to have a family business. Which of these apply to you?

- **Perception of being in control of destiny** – because you are privately owned there is little or no pressure from the share markets or takeover risk.

- **Potential high rewards** – fortunes can be, and are, made in family businesses. Over one-third of the Fortune 500 are still family businesses. And many of the rewards are non-monetary – family can support a person's sense of identity through the business.

- **Independence to take a long-term view** – you are answerable only to the family shareholders and not to an external group of interests, so you can do what the business needs rather than be driven by the next half-year report.

- **Family culture can be a source of pride, stability, commitment and continuity** – there is a level of loyalty and trust in families that is difficult to surpass (when working well!). Family businesses are also a great way for a young person to have a head start in life.

- **Willingness to reinvest** – it's ours, we know the business and we are willing to put our money on the line.

- **Family members' expertise in the sector** – usually members of the family are deeply embedded in and know a great deal about the industry, be it farming, horticulture, trucking, retail, law, etc.

- **Flexibility** – family businesses give the owners a great deal of choice about their lives, their involvement in the business and about timing issues.

Challenges ... and then some

It's not all easy. Family businesses face all of the usual business issues (such as access to capital, pressure on profits, cash flow problems, customer service hassles, staffing difficulties) as well as some specific challenges. Which ones do you have?

- balancing the needs of family and the needs of business
- sibling rivalry
- intergenerational conflict
- incomplete skill sets
- lack of management depth
- hiring in …
- … and firing family members
- key employees who are not family
- succession
- other _____

It is common for family disputes to overflow into the business and affect performance. All people define themselves by their work and their family – merge the two and you have a potent cocktail. These tensions are as old as Cain and Abel!

Too many hats

One of the complications in a family business is that any one individual may have several different roles. Each will require a different perspective on what is happening. An issue may cause conflict between the different roles. Each of these roles brings different responsibilities and requires a different mindset. You need to decide: which hat do you wear?

The roles may or may not overlap: e.g. you might be a shareholder in the business and/or a member of the family and/or an employee of the business.

Imagine the conflicts presented by a dividend policy. Person A might want to increase dividends while Person B might prefer reinvestment leading to expansion of the business and better career opportunities. And A and B may be siblings!

It is very important that everyone knows which hats they wear and which voice should be speaking at any time. There is a lot of potential for poor business practice and conflict between individuals when people forget which role they should be playing at any meeting or in any conversation or decision.

Management v. ownership

It's very important to make these lines clear. Shareholders often feel that ownership gives them management rights. This kind of interference in the business can be disastrous. Imagine four siblings with 25% shareholding each but none of them with the authority of the managing shareholder! The problems can be even worse if you have non-shareholding managers (external professional managers) who are being countermanded by family members at every turn. If they are any good they won't stay and the business will have lost a very valuable resource. Professional managers are often very reluctant to work for a family business for exactly this reason. Smart ones do their research on the family's behaviour to avoid being caught in such a situation, so make sure that the good ones will choose you.

Non-family employees – loyal retainers or servants?

Family businesses can easily fall into the trap of treating non-family members poorly. All employees want the same things, whether it's a family business or not. You will need to attract and retain good staff. Can you tick the box on these features:

- earn a fair wage
- profit share
- retirement programmes
- benefits – insurance, childcare
- training and development
- career opportunity
- involvement in decisions
- security.

Rules for hiring relatives

There are very good reasons for hiring family members.

After all, looking after your family is probably one of the main reasons you are in a family business. However, everything that can go wrong with recruitment and selection of employees applies – and then some (see Finding Great People – page 216). Some additional 'rules' to keep in mind include:

- **Same/better standards of performance apply.** Don't accept anything less. Family members should be at least as good as external candidates. Your non-family employees will be watching closely.

- **No favouritism.** Apply the same rules, e.g. regarding timekeeping, dress codes, menial jobs, travel allowances, etc.

- **Treat them fairly.** They are not slave labour. Many young people flee family farms and other businesses as the deal anywhere else is better! This is the exact opposite of what their family wanted and is all too frequently the tragic outcome of bad management.

- **Restrict socialising to after work.** While at work it is best to treat all employees equally.

- **Avoid family issues at work.**

- **Make promotional standards clear.** You are not doing your business – or your relative – any favours by promoting them if they are not good enough. Be clear about the criteria and make sure that everyone can see that the person has earned their position. Overachieving would be even better – it should be harder to get promoted if you are the boss's son or daughter.

Family members are family members 24/7. There are pros and cons about working alongside family. On the one hand you may have a great deal of knowledge and understanding about each other that you can use to complement each other well at work. You may also be willing to go the extra mile for family members – after all you may be able to get more money elsewhere but where will you get another parent or brother or sister? However, home is home and a job is a job. Be aware of how the family and business interconnect and where a line has to be drawn.

Do your best to minimise any negative effects on either the family or the business. You need to run the business with your head and not your heart. Different standards of performance apply around your dinner table than around the board table. Give plenty of thought to how relationships and tolerances need to play out differently in the workplace.

Succession is the ultimate test

Families often avoid succession issues. It often requires an emergency – death, disability or other disaster – to trigger a discussion. Succession is avoided because:

- It raises difficult family issues – such as who will (or won't) succeed.

- It forces people to confront their own mortality.

- The boss is too busy on day-to-day tasks – and prefers them!

- The boss fears a loss of control.

- The business is 'my life' or 'my nest egg'.

- There is a fear that a succession plan will reduce options.

- They don't know how to plan for succession.

Make your kids fit for the job

It's natural to love your kids. Unfortunately it's also 'natural' to both underdo and overdo the things that will make them competent to take their place in the family business. You need to remember the points listed below.

- **Avoid overindulgence.** Business owners naturally want to reward themselves and their family for all the hard work. This can lead to a lavish lifestyle or the indulgence of children. Be careful about making it too easy. They need to learn to strive and also to be financially prudent – after all, they'll be in charge of the chequebook some day soon.

- **Opportunities for learning**. Give your kids the chance to make some mistakes – and learn from them. If they are not making any, what they are doing is too easy and you need to stretch them. On the other hand, it is not wise to give them responsibility way beyond their competence or judgement.

- **Starting at the bottom.** No job is too menial. It's

important to learn the family business from the ground up. In addition non-family staff members appreciate seeing the young ones earn their position – and this helps get rid of later jealousies when your kids have proved themselves and are moved into senior positions.

- **Sending them away.** The world is bigger than your business. Your kids will be managing your family business in a different world in the future. It's a good idea to give them experiences in other worlds – other places, other businesses where they can develop themselves without either the advantages, or the pressures, of being the boss's kids. They will return if it's right for them and the business.

- **Paying market rates.** No more, no less. That's fair to everyone and it's sound business practice.

- **Managing performance professionally.** Position description, performance standards, lots (and lots!) of feedback. If you have senior non-family professionals they may be well suited to this – but they'll need to be both very good and very secure in their roles. Parents are likely to be overindulgent or overly harsh. You may need to consider an external coach or mentor to get the best results. It's worth it – you have a lot riding on a good outcome.

You need to work on your organisation to build a wealth-creating asset. If you want to build a great business you must find loyal customers and hire great people. In Section Three, we look at 'Other People – Customers and Employees'.

SECTION 3: OTHER PEOPLE – CUSTOMERS AND EMPLOYEES

Success in business is all about other people. First of all, there are the customers or clients – without them there is no business. Then there are the people who work with you – employees, contractors and agents. Successful business owners work hard to harness the motivation of others so that everyone wins. It takes a lot of empathy to succeed – you have to put a great deal of effort into understanding others and treating them in a way that builds good long-term relationships. Successful people are good at recognising others' contributions and making them feel good about themselves. These kinds of people have lots of energy and the ability to energise others so that we all succeed.

It's a lifelong job to be great with others. It's most important to start with attracting great staff and loyal customers and this is what we address in this section.

FINDING CUSTOMERS AND KEEPING THEM

Customers and their worlds are changing all the time. Once you find a customer you must work hard to keep them. Your business has to keep up; what worked for your customers last year (and sometimes even *last week*!) may not work next time.

Killer Question

What's the unique buying proposition?

In other words, are you clear about what your business offers that makes it meet the needs of your target customers better than your competitors? It could be quality or price or convenience or an agency you hold or a relationship you have built or staff you have retained or your location or hours of operation or after-sales service or expertise or your online offering or speed among other things.

There needs to be something the customer values that you do better than the rest or that would make it hard for them to switch to another business. You need to know what this is so you can amplify, promote and leverage it. *What are you going to be terrific at in the eyes of your customers?*

Killer Question

If you were one of your competitors, what could you do in the next five years to wipe out this business?

Your competitor may already be working on implementing this strategy. Get there first and make sure you're always more than one step ahead of them!

Segment the market

You can't target everybody. Even if you have a vast array of customers you will need to think about them as distinct groups or segments. Each segment will be driven by different things, e.g. when purchasing food, young singles want convenience/on the run, young couples want fashion, young families want value, older people want small portions/nutrition. You will need to profile each segment you serve so that you fully understand them, what they want and how you will meet their needs. The better you understand the segment the easier it is to market to more of them, i.e. get a bigger share of the young professionals segment in your region, for example. Your people may find it fun to name each segment – it helps people to really think about the attributes of the segment. Build a profile for each segment:

- likes
- dislikes
- needs
- concerns
- buying patterns.

Then analyse each segment to see how you can grow sales with them:

- What does the customer do?
- What else will they want?
- What are the real benefits of our product/service to them and can any of our benefits/advantages meet any of their needs?

Segments are getting smaller. In some markets, you will have to deal with 'segments of one' – i.e. every customer/client is different and will expect you to accommodate that, e.g. planning a wedding or customising a mountain bike.

EXAMPLE

A dry-cleaner observed his customers over time and analysed his accounts. He noticed that he had three distinct segments – commercial customers like hotels, family customers and busi-

nesspeople. Different things were important to each group: mothers were price sensitive and responded well to deals on dry-cleaning school uniforms at the end of term and to seasonal deals for cleaning duvets, curtains, furniture covers, etc. Commercial clients wanted discounts for volume, needed pick-up and delivery services and needed seven-day-a-week operations. Businesspeople were heavy users, were not price sensitive and wanted same day service. Convenient location and parking facilities were important to them. Pick-up and return to their office was a winning strategy.

What is the customer buying?

This is not an easy question to answer. You might be selling drills, but the customer does not want a drill – the customer is buying a hole! A car salesperson is clearly selling cars, but the customer may be buying school transport or prestige or sex! It's the same with services – you might be selling advice, but the customer is purchasing security or wealth or advancement or revenge! People don't buy products (features). They buy what products do (advantages).

Different people want the product to do different things (benefits to *them*). Ask yourself:

- What are customers buying when they buy from you?
- Do your sales and service people understand these needs?

- What can you do to find out more about your customers' needs and desires?

Hunt for unmet needs

The fancy name for this is market intelligence! That can cover a multitude of things. But you can never be too close to what is going on. Many business people spend far too much time working on today's stuff rather than hunting out tomorrow. What will your customers want next? What are the competition already doing? What's happening in other industries? What are younger people into? You have to get out there, walk the streets, visit places your customers go, read the trade journals that apply in your area, look at what's happening overseas in your industry, search the internet, read blogs and find out what's happening at the edges of your market. Most importantly, you have no business if you are not servicing the needs/wants/desires of customers and so it pays to research the market for unmet needs.

Some detective work to consider:

- Go to the movies.
- Read your kids' magazines.
- Listen to your teenagers – what's hot?
- Read some stuff that upsets you!
- Walk the streets – what are other people doing differently that might work in your business?
- Travel around the country or overseas.

- Research what Enterprise Ireland and Venture Capitalists and other investors are currently funding.
- Surf the web.
- Subscribe to internet trend-watching sites.
- Join relevant online groups.
- Read the papers.
- Listen to business programmes on radio.
- Look at what's happening in different industries.
- Find out what customers are demanding – and getting – elsewhere in their lives.
- Benchmark, e.g. if Amazon can send it from the US in three days, why do we take three weeks to deliver something? And what if our competitors become more efficient before we do?
- 'Crash' your business into other businesses in other industries, e.g. if I ran my business like a Formula One team (speed, accuracy, precision, etc.), what would it be like and would I meet any other customer needs?

Think about all of the things people spend money on today that they did not twenty years ago (hire-a-hubby, prenuptial agreements, purchasing anything and everything online, mobile phones, bottled water, coffee and hot food at the garage!) and consider where things might be headed in your industry.

Remember, the principles of marketing have remained relatively static for fifty years, but the target of marketing (i.e. the customer) and the routes to them are changing at an accelerating rate. Your business must keep up with these changes – or someone else will eat your lunch.

The Customers are the real boss. They have the power to fire every employee, from the Chairman down!

Sam Walton, Walmart

Growth is the objective

Marketing is about markets and your products/services. You only have a limited number of choices – you either have to sell more of the same or develop new things to sell. Your choices look like this:

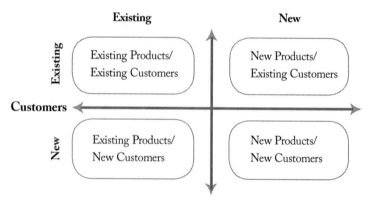

These choices are not all equal. It is usually easiest to sell more of what you have to your existing customers. The next easiest is to find new customers and the most likely are people just like your existing customers. New products and services raise the risk level – you can never tell if they will work. The riskiest of all is to attempt to develop new products for customers you don't yet have – this is the equivalent of a new business!

This model is a useful way to plot marketing strategy – fill in the boxes and look at your options in each. Explore the easiest and less risky options first, i.e. can you get your existing customers to use more or find more customers just like them?

EXAMPLE

These are the choices for growth considered by a printing business:

Example for a Printing Business

Products/Services

	Existing	New
Existing Customers	**1** Sell more business cards to existing customers – perhaps by persuading them to have different colours or designs.	**2** Target your customers for personalised printed stationery: greeting cards, notepaper, stickers and envelopes.
New	**3** Sell business cards to people not in business – just as a convenience that people can use any time.	**4** Target schools to print artwork as posters for fund-raising purposes.

Quadrant 1: It should not be too difficult to get existing customers to consume more by offering several colours or some cards with photos or generic cards for the business.

Quadrant 2: These existing customers should be relatively easy to up-sell to compliment slips, special occasion cards or envelopes printed with their logo.

Quadrant 3: New customers might be more of the same business people (greater market share) or quite different people like mums who constantly have to write down their address and phone number for other parents.

Quadrant 4: It is a novel idea to target schools to use print for a fund-raiser. It might work but would probably take quite a lot of work and it would make better business sense to explore the other options for growth first.

Listen until it hurts!

Talk with and listen to everyone who is connected with your business. You'll be amazed at what you find out. That does not mean that you have to act on everything you hear, e.g. the sales reps always think that the price is too high! Survey some or all of your customers. You can do this anonymously, cheaply and speedily online using tools such as Surveymonkey.com. Again, 'buyers are always liars' – not everything you hear will be valid. But that's no reason not to ask. Focus groups (small) of suppliers or clients often throw up some very interesting ideas – at the very least you will find out some things you did not know. It often helps to use an external facilitator – they may not want to tell you in person what they *really* think! Put on some drinks for ten of your customers and ask:

- What do we do well that is important to you?

- What do we do poorly that is important to you?

- What do we do that you do not need?

- What do we not do that you need us to do?

- What problems do *you* have satisfying your customers?

- What problems do you have doing business with us?

- How do we compare with other businesses you deal with?

- What things do we do that make no sense to you?

- Will you buy from us again? If yes, why? If not, why not?

You are looking for ideas to help you determine what you need to *start* doing, *stop* doing and *keep* doing! These three categories are a great way to start your marketing plan. And everyone in the business will be able to contribute ideas in each category.

Helping Customers to Buy

Purchases are what count!

It doesn't really matter what you are selling – what matters is that people buy! Nothing happens until someone buys something. Your business success rests on the amount of products or services that are purchased. If your sales are good it is easy to address the other problems in your business; if your sales are poor almost nothing will save you. It is very tempting to keep looking at selling from your point of view. What really makes the difference is approaching sales from the purchaser's point of view. Make your customers successful – help them buy what they need to solve their problem. Make sure you help your clients to win – and you will too. While every industry and every business has different products and services, the principles of selling are the same. And selling more will make a bigger difference to your business than anything else. Remember: *If it isn't good for the customer, it isn't good for you.*

Killer Question

Why should anyone buy from YOU?

What is it about your product or service that is attractive to the customer? If it is the same as other products/services, what is it about your customer service, your people, your location, your premises, your after-sales support, your terms of trade, your accessibility, or your hours of business that make your product more attractive for the purchaser?

Know your stuff!

No matter what you are selling you (and your people) need to understand the product or service well. You will need to be able to discuss the features and advantages of whatever you sell. Are you and your people good at explaining:

- What it is
- What it does for purchasers (the benefits to them)
- How it operates
- What it can do to help
- What it costs
- Terms of trade
- Warranties and guarantees
- After-sales service arrangements
- Delivery options.

If your product or service is at all complicated it may need to be supported by written material like brochures, a website, Facebook page or blog.

Seven steps to successful selling

1. **Research the target customers** – Who are they? Where are they? How will you reach them? How will you meet them or attract them to your premises?

2. **Set objectives for each encounter** – What are you attempting to achieve on each contact or meeting? What outcome do you want?

3. **Uncover individual needs** – What questions will you need to ask to find out their problems, their motivations, their unmet needs?

4. **Present solutions** – What features and advantages have you to offer? Can you tailor these as benefits to each customer.

5. **Overcome resistance** – What objections are you likely to meet? What strategies have you got to overcome these objections?

6. **Negotiate** – Where have you room to move, what can you offer to advance the sale?

7. **Close the sale** – How will you ask for the sale? How will you conclude and take action on the purchase?

FAB sales

Customers and clients buy benefits – they buy whatever it is that your product or service will do *for them*. Less able salespeople sell features – they focus on what the product or service does. They may even do this in a very polished and professional way. If they have worked hard on their skills they may even sell the advantages of the product or service. But the customer is not interested; the customer is looking for the benefit – what the product or service will give to that individual.

To sell benefits you have to work hard on figuring out what each customer's 'problem' is. For example, if you are selling a car, is the customer looking for transport for the family? Security in the form of safety? Economical travel? Reliable transport? Status? To look good? To appear younger? To seem successful? To attract the opposite sex?

The acronym FAB (Feature, Advantage, Benefit) is useful in making the leap from understanding the features of your product or service to understanding the benefits that you can sell to your customer. It is easy to learn to FAB your products or services:

EXAMPLE

Sunscreen:

- **Feature:** Sunny Sunscreen has an SPF of 45.

- **Advantage:** This will allow you to spend a long time outdoors safely.

- **Benefit to CUSTOMER:** As YOU are a keen walker, this means your fair skin will be well protected for several hours between applications.

EXAMPLE

Home Help Services:

- **Feature:** Our business has over forty cleaners, gardeners and handy persons.

- **Advantage:** We can provide a full service to your home.

- **Benefit to CUSTOMER:** As YOU travel frequently we can provide a home management service to meet any of your needs – whenever you want, whether you are at home or overseas.

EXERCISE

You will already know the features and advantages of the products and services that you sell. Take a group of your customers and work out what the benefits are for each customer. This is a great exercise to do with other people in your business.

Buyers are liars!

Do you know why your customers are purchasing your products or services? You must listen to the customer/client but you should be aware that customers and clients often don't admit to their real reason for purchase. This is because most purchases are made on an emotional basis. Potential purchasers justify their decision to buy within their heads – and give others 'logical' reasons for their decisions.

You will need to continue to study your market to understand the real motivations behind the interest in your product or service. Ask yourself: why are they buying?

They are buying you

In many businesses there is very little difference between the products and services you are offering and those of your competitors. This often means that it is you (and the others in your business) who makes the difference. In many cases, customers are buying your business, its brand, its reputation and the way in which you conduct yourself. Do your customers like you? Are you helpful? Do you follow up? Do you target the right product/ service to the right customers? Can you give additional advice and support? Can you make suggestions about the use of your product or service? Are you truthful and dependable? When people have a choice they do business with people they like. Are you someone they like? Are the other people in your business likeable?

Words and phrases that sell

The words and phrases that you use on and off-line – in speech, on notices, billboards, windows, blackboards, direct marketing copy and brochures – are critical. You have minimal time to attract people's attention and communicate your message. Below is a list of words and phrases that attract people's attention, and when you've got their attention you're halfway to making a sale.

Words that sell	Phrases that sell
• free	• trial offer
• new	• thousands of satisfied customers
• easy	• no deposit
• win	• — days interest free
• you	• buy one, get one free
• save	• money back guarantee
• fast	• same day delivery
• yes	• finance arranged
• sale	• it really works
• guaranteed	• you deserve it
• love	• the standard setter

Assess your sales skills (or get your team to assess theirs)

EXERCISE

Look at the statements below and tick the appropriate box that applies to you, then add up the totals in each column.

	Statement	Always	Sometimes	Never
1	I plan before I approach prospects.			
2	I have a specific objective for each call or contact.			

3	I prepare carefully before a meeting.			
4	I have good questions to ask.			
5	I work at learning new skills.			
6	I study the customers to find out what they want.			
7	I keep good records about customers.			
8	I listen carefully to what they say.			
9	I try to put myself in the purchaser's shoes.			
10	I always find out who can make the decision.			
11	I structure my presentations carefully.			
12	I present features and advantages thoroughly.			
13	I choose and present the right benefits.			
14	I return all calls within twenty-four hours.			
15	I do whatever I say I'll do.			
16	I keep notes on each contact with the customer.			
17	I keep in touch with my customers regularly.			

18	I handle objections constructively.			
19	I negotiate to get agreement.			
20	I always try to close the sale.			

How many ticks did you have in the always column?

- 0–10 – You have a lot of skills to learn!

- 10–15 – You are on the right track to success.

- 15–20 – You are well on the way to being a superior salesperson.

The 80/20 rule revisited!

Let's revisit the 80/20 rule we used to examine ourselves in Section 1. How can we apply this to sales and to our customers?

- Which 20% of customers account for 80% of sales?

- Which 20% of salespeople make 80% of the sales?

- Which 20% of products account for 80% of profits?

- Which 20% of products/customers/salespeople account for 80% of problems?

- Which 20% of activities lead to 80% of results?

A small change in focus could bring very great rewards.

You Have Only One Reputation: Building Your Brand

Killer Questions

How is your business (brand) perceived?

How do you need your business (brand) to be perceived?

Brands win

You may not feel that your business is in a heavily 'branded' industry – you might be running a panel-beating operation rather than marketing chocolate bars – but don't be deceived. You may even think that all branding is about advertising hype and has little substance. But brands are everything. And you *do* have a brand. *You* may even be the brand yourself – when the customer or client hires you, what is the brand they are buying? What do they think and feel when they hear your name? What is your brand saying? What does it mean to the customer? Are you managing your brand well? If you aren't clear about the brand you want to portray, potential customers will fill in the gaps for you and create your brand in their minds and it may not be the one you want. Be sure to think through the brand you want. Remember, Coca-Cola didn't win the blind taste test and Microsoft may not have the best operating system, but brands win. A brand is much more than just the product itself or what it does. Try to avoid the trap of thinking of marketing and branding as something separate from the business – marketing and branding *are* the business.

What is the brand?

At the most basic level a brand is a name, term, design, symbol, or any other feature that identifies one seller's goods or service as distinct from those of other sellers. Branding began as a way to tell one person's cattle from another by means of a hot iron stamp. It is the personality that identifies a product, service or company (name, term, sign, symbol, design, or a combination of these) and how it relates to key constituencies: customers.

A brand is really what your company *means* to the prospective customer. The brand is what the prospective customer *thinks* you are. If it means something good to the prospective customer it means money to the business owner. The brand is the *package of value* that the customer thinks you offer. Your brand is your *reputation* and it should be nurtured and guarded well. A well-managed, strong brand will incorporate all of the things in the diagram above.

Killer Questions

If people are buying You, are you really clear about what brand 'you' is saying?

When was the last time you Googled yourself and what did you find?

Brand You

It is often You (and your team) who make the difference and cause customers to buy. Brand You is why people choose you or not. Are you clear about what your different personas are communicating? With the advancement of business online, you need to be really clear as to how you want yourself and your business to be perceived. We all have multiple personas online:

- Personal persona – keep this private to yourself, family and close friends.

- You as a business person – ensure you want to be who Google says you are.
- Your company brand – you, your company, your colleagues.

It is important that you are clear about who you want to be seen to be by your customers and that you are who you say you are online. To help create your online persona, the three things that search engines love are:

1 Say what you do in text (whether you're a plumber in North County Dublin or a glass-blower in West Cork).

2 Keep online content active by updating it – if you don't update your persona online Google thinks you're dead.

3 Create links – decide what your personas are and link them all together through the likes of LinkedIn, website, blogs, Twitter, Facebook, etc.

Questions for defining the brand

- Who are you?
- What do you do?
- What are the things the business is good at?
- What can you really deliver on – where is the business really capable?
- What do you want to be famous for?

- What can you offer that the prospective customer values – unique products or services, lower costs/prices, superior skills/experience, better customer service, a broader choice of products or comprehensive services, a one-stop shop, speedy delivery …?

You may have to make some hard choices. For example, some businesses are all over the place and do whatever work presents itself. You may need to become clearer about what you do and whom you serve. If you currently have a 'job' but want to create a 'business', be clear about what brand you'd like to have, i.e. what do you want to come to your customer's mind when they think of your business? The example below shows how a professional services firm might choose between different areas of business in order to better define their brand:

Professional Practice Branding Choices

Pure Generalist

- Wide Range of Services to Clients

Pure Specialist

- Narrow Range of Services to Narrow Range of Clients

Narrow Market Specialist

- Wide Range of Services to Narrow Range of Clients

Wide Market Specialist

- Narrow Range of Services to Variety of Clients

The answers to the questions above tell you how to define your brand, e.g. 'we provide a one-stop family law service for our local community', 'we offer premium design and printing products and services for Limerick', 'we fix PC problems – *fast!*' Your brand definition is for internal purposes – it is not necessarily what you will say to the prospective customer or what you will put in your advertising. However, you – and all of your people – need to be clear about your brand definition.

EXAMPLE

Lidl is a discount store. Their premises are large, (often) standalone, purpose-built retail units and the layout and merchandising is very basic. The staff are all tidily but informally dressed. The slogan is 'Quality for less'. It is clear that the pitch is value/low price and everything else lines up to emphasise that message. The day you go in there and find carpeted floors is the day you know that they have 'lost the plot' and a marketing disaster is around the corner.

By contrast, if you visit a BMW showroom, where the pitch is upmarket and exclusive, you will expect plush furnishing, suited salespeople and so on. A concrete floor would send a very inappropriate message.

Brand positioning

Positioning starts with your product or service or business – you have to have something to attain the desired position. Positioning is the effect you want to have on the mind of the prospective customer, i.e. where you want your offering to be positioned in his mind. Should it be filed under Quality? Cheap? Luxury? Reliable? Desirable? Dependable? Speed? Innovation?

Keys to successful positioning:

- Be as different as you can, e.g. 'Hire a Hubby' concept and name.
- Be consistent and send the same message every time, e.g. 'Where everyone gets a bargain!'
- Ensure everything fits your position, e.g. logo, van, slogan, name, online presence, uniform.

Brand appearance

You also need to manage the physical presentation or look of your brand. Alignment matters. Work to make sure that everything lines up. Check the look across your:

- product
- logo
- packaging
- online presence
- business cards
- signage
- vehicles

- billboards
- stationery
- graphics
- advertising
- promotions
- merchandising materials
- trade show materials and booths
- gift items
- apparel
- public relations
- written reports.

You don't need to spend a fortune on this, but if you look at your current brand and you know it isn't correctly representing your business, it'll save you money in the long term to use a professional designer (get referrals from others). If you have to keep changing things, such as your colours, logo or slogan, it will cost you a lot and is also very confusing for your customers. Make sure that the designers you choose have done some of this kind of work before and that it looks good to you. You are trying to send a *consistent* message to your prospective customers, e.g. everything about Lidl communicates low price/value, from the retail unit to the boxes to the concrete floor.

Perceptions matter

How does each of your key stakeholder groups see your product or service or total business (including you and your colleagues)? Map their perceptions. It does not matter whether these are 'fair' or whether you agree with them or not: perception is reality.

What matters? How do you rate?

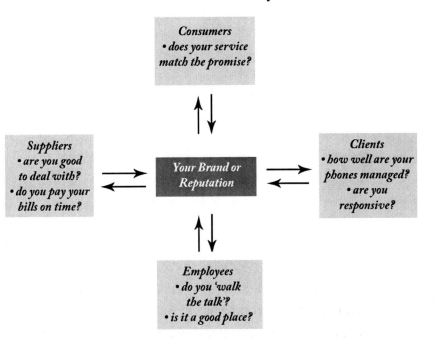

You can then map the perceptions that you need them to have in order for your product, service or total business to be successful – to gain market share, to have loyal customers and clients, to charge premium prices, to have high margins, and to attract and retain good employees.

EXERCISE

What perceptions do key stakeholders need to have about you, your products and services and your overall business in order for your business to be successful?

What perceptions do they need to have?

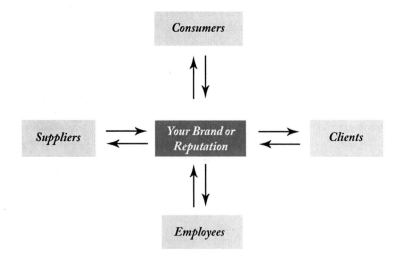

Manage their perceptions

Uncontrolled perceptions will damage your brand. Your brand is communicating all the time, whether you are spending money on marketing communications or not, e.g. how your staff answer the phone. In any case, what you do and the experience customers or clients have of you 'shouts' so loud that they will never hear what you are saying through marketing communications anyway – they must complement each other. The essence of the brand is what you and your team actually deliver and how you do everything that you do. Does it all align with what you want the brand to mean and what you want the customers to feel about your brand?

Example	Good perception	Poor perception
You sell expensive interior design and furnishings	Your delivery person takes off his shoes in the client's house and polishes everything he installs	Your delivery person turns up in an old battered vehicle
You are presenting to a client's board of directors	You are early, impeccably groomed and provide hand-outs of your presentation	You barely make it on time and appear to be seeing your own presentation for the first time!
You run a busy café	Your food is well presented and your staff are clean and smart	You have overflowing rubbish bins and your staff are smoking in clear view outside

EXAMPLE

The explosion of online communications makes brand building more exciting than ever, as well as more challenging. Be clear about what you want to communicate and have an internal policy on social media usage by your team.

Build your brand internally

You are relying on everyone in the business to deliver on the brand. Make sure they understand what you believe the business to be about and the position you want to have in the minds of your customers. Then help them make sure that everything they do reinforces this perception. If your own people don't believe in the product, service or business (or you!), then they are unlikely to give the customer the experience of dealing with your business that you want. Internal branding is key to successful brand building. You need your people to turn the promises your brand is making into a reality for your customers. Everything you do every day in the business either adds to the brand or detracts from it.

Live the Brand, Every Day, In Every Way.

Money in the bank

Brands attract a premium. A good brand attracts a higher price. Just take a tour of the supermarket and compare own brands with branded products. Then look at the premium price that the strongest brand in each category commands. Brands build your wealth in several ways. The habit of consumer brand loyalty makes a good brand worth a lot of on-going money. Loyalty is very profitable. In addition, a strong brand provides some stability against new entrants into your market – the stronger the brand the more unlikely they are to take you on at all and it takes a great offer to make customers shift from a brand they love. Trust matters and in the services market it is usually enough to keep the client for a lifetime unless you breach the trust in some way. Strong brands always get listed – the shop or the pub or the hardware store has to carry them in the interest of their own business.

Cash flow is very important to your business and everyone is looking to enhance this in the short term. However, building your brand is about longer-term value – both the sale value of the business and ensuring good cash flows in the medium and long term. A good brand that customers trust to give value/be reliable/give fast service, and that they continue to purchase, is money in the bank.

Brand equity

Brands have value. It is often difficult to quantify the value of the brand, though some businesses are so confident of their brand value, for example Coca-Cola, that they put the value of the brand on the balance sheet. However, the intangible value of your brand will contribute to the goodwill your business may attract over and above the value of the tangible assets of the business. Brand equity is made up of things like brand name awareness, brand loyalty, perceived quality of the brand and the associations that go with the brand. It reflects the premium that people will pay and the probability that they will continue to purchase.

EXERCISE

Set targets for your brand. Are you building a high brand equity/high margin business or a price-driven commodity business? How much should the brand be worth in five years time (sale value)? What should your business know about branding/marketing?

Brands help people choose

Purchase isn't rational, i.e. people buy on price only when all other things are relatively equal. All washing machines wash, all jeans are hard wearing, all detergents remove grease ... so why do we consistently choose some over others. All solicitors and accountants have degrees and professional qualifications, all the plumbers did their apprenticeship and necessary trade exams. When faced with the huge range of choices we have – twenty varieties of jams, jeans, juice – we turn for reassurance and comfort to something we know and trust and like.

The best brands hook into our emotions. They appeal to our various senses and they engender a sense of trust and dependability. So we continue to buy Heinz baked beans, Kellogg's cornflakes, Colgate toothpaste. People may not need what you offer often, but you need to manage your brand so that they are likely to think of you and turn in your direction when they do.

Brand slogans

Good slogans – if we believe them – can help define and reinforce a brand. Lidl's 'Quality for less' not only tells us what the store is about, but also reinforces our sense of value. Slogans convey important reasons to use the brand – Nike's 'Just Do It' reminds us that their products are about activity and fitness and participation, Apple's 'Think Different' reminds us they are all about innovation.

> *Who steals my purse steals trash; ... But he that filches from me my good name ... makes me poor indeed.*
>
> Othello, *William Shakespeare*

Handling Complaints

Killer Question

Complaints are a gift so how do I get them to complain?

Startling service statistics

- Fewer than two in ten who are unhappy complain. You just never hear about the other 80%.

- Dissatisfied customers tell up to twenty others about their problem.

- More than 75% of customers who have their complaint resolved satisfactorily will do business with you again.

Make it easy to complain

It is in your interests to hear when customers are unhappy because complaints:

- give you a chance to rescue the situation with that customer.

- allow you to show that your pledges and guarantees actually mean something.

- provide an early warning system of things that are not working well and that could become very damaging to your business.

- expose aspects of your business that are not working for customers and give you a chance to change.

- give you an opportunity to impress a customer by how well you respond to the complaint (a customer who has a complaint that is well handled often becomes an even better customer).

Welcome complaints – there are no trading activities that do not depend on repeat business. Complaints show you what you need to change to get repeat business.

Reasons you may receive complaints

Which of the following is the most likely cause of complaints about your business?

- Defective products.

- Services that don't deliver what is promised.

- Poor quality – only partial or patchy delivery of the offer.

- Uncaring staff – bad attitude.

- Poor staff training – they don't know what's expected of them.

- Differences between what the business thinks customers want and what the customers really want.

- No customer service philosophy or policy in the business.

- Poor handling of problems.

- Staff have no authority to take responsibility.

- Staff are not allowed to make decisions that solve customer problems.

Handling complaints well

- **Have a procedure** so that your staff know what to do whenever they receive a complaint.

- **Have a 'no blame' culture** so that staff will feel confident and secure about dealing with complaints. If not they will cover them up when they can. The focus needs to be on fixing the problem, not on pointing the finger.

- **Have a sense of urgency** about resolving the problem for the customer. The analysis can wait until later.

- **Have a commitment to over recover** so that the customer goes away more impressed than ever. Complaints give you an opportunity to deliver a 'wow' performance.

- **Have a position on satisfaction** so that customers know that you back your products or services, e.g. that you offer a money-back guarantee or 100% satisfaction. This will attract custom and will probably justify higher prices.

The customer is not always right but ...

The customer is not always right but the customer is always the customer. Customers can be wrong. They may even have caused some of the problem. Sometimes you may even suspect them of dishonesty. However, you will never win an argument with a customer. Try to avoid unpleasantness and work hard at establishing what has gone wrong. Then get busy on putting things right as quickly as possible. Even when you think the customer is wrong it is usually not worth risking bad publicity. Never give the customer a reason to leave.

Never say 'no' – find a way to say 'yes'

No customer should ever be told:

- Go to another office.
- Call another number.
- Phone back tomorrow.
- You will have to ...
- We can't do that.

Customers and clients don't like hearing the 'no' word. The customer or client is looking for a solution and they usually just tell you what they want you to do to resolve the problem. The solution they request is often something that you cannot provide. The trick is to find out what the problem really is because there is often a solution that you *can* offer. Try to find out more, e.g. 'So why would you like us to …?' Then you can follow with your own offer, e.g. 'If I could do X would that work for you?' Once you fully understand the issue you may well have a variety of solutions you can offer and avoid the dreaded 'no'! Customers want to hear what you *can* do or *will* do. Some businesses go further: employees have authority to say 'yes' to a customer, but if they want to say 'no' they have to ask permission!

Ten deadly sins

You may not say these words, but your tone or attitude can have the same effect:

1.   I don't know.

2.   I don't care.

3.   I can't be bothered.

4.   I don't like you.

5.   I am the expert.

6.   You don't know anything.

7.   We don't want your kind here.

8.   Don't come back.

9.   I'm right, you're wrong.

10. Hurry up and wait.

Five steps to recovery

1. **Apologise.** Say sorry for whatever has upset them. Try to sound as sincere as possible. Take responsibility for trying to resolve whatever the problem is. For example, 'I am really sorry you are upset. I will do whatever I can to fix the problem.' Never blame another staff member.

2. **Clarify.** Check that you really understand what the customer is unhappy about. Ask questions and then try to restate what they have said: 'So when your business cards finally arrived three days later than agreed, the cell phone number was incorrect. Is that right?' It is very important that you understand the exact nature of the problem.

3. **Empathise.** Show you understand that they are unhappy. Be careful not to minimise their complaint (e.g. 'Is that all?') or to patronise. It is much better to say something neutral like 'I can see why you are upset.'

4. **Recover.** List the possible solutions, e.g. 'Well, I can get you another one or I can give you a full refund.' Take action. Depending on the complaint and your business, you may need to offer a refund, provide a new product, redo the service, or offer a complimentary additional product or service. The faster you can take action the better. Recovery may cost you money, but it is money well spent. The cost of not recovering well can be great – others are told, your reputation suffers and you may lose a valuable lifetime customer.

5. **Follow up.** The best businesses follow up. At the time they check that the complaint has been resolved – 'Is everything OK now? Have we done what you need to fix the problem? Will you be happy if I organise that?' Even better is a further follow up a few days later – a phone call or a letter. If appropriate, some free product or a gift certificate for your service is a nice additional gesture. The point is to recover so well that you have created a very loyal customer.

Retaining by recovering well

Bad things happen in all businesses. From time to time you will have to deal with customers or clients who are dissatisfied, unhappy and even upset with your products or services. However, if you handle problems and complaints well, customers are typically even more impressed with you than if there had never been a difficulty. It is a good idea to have a policy in place so that the staff know exactly how to deal with the different types of issue that may arise, as in this example.

Policy	Procedure	Satisfy by:
Returns	Ask questions to establish if the product was faulty, or unsuitable, or if the customer just changed their mind.	Offering another product, offering to order a different product, offering a full refund. The customer decides.

Using complaints to build a better business

Log all of your complaints under the headings on a table like the one below.

When	Who	What	Action taken	Comments

At regular intervals (e.g. quarterly) you should analyse the complaints log and see what needs to be done to build a better and more profitable business. Your complaints log might identify:

- A particular product that is causing dissatisfaction – Badly made? Poorly stored? Problem with distributor?

- A particular staff member who is the occasion of complaints – Attitude? Lack of product knowledge? Over-enthusiastic selling? Poor training?

- A particular outlet – Have you a problem in one location?

- A breakdown in the chain of delivery – Are we getting most things right but dropping the ball at a crucial point? Do people understand *internal* customer service and how to manage handovers?

Analysing complaints data

Gathering complaints information helps you make rational decisions and prevents you overreacting (and spending money) on the wrong things.

Graphing data allows you to see where most of the problems are occurring. You can also use it to see how much complaints are costing your business to fix.

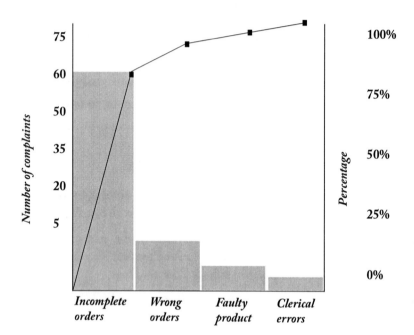

The above diagram shows that 90% of the cost of fixing complaints comes from incomplete orders and wrong orders for this business (another application of Pareto!). Knowing where most of your problems are can save you a lot of money and time when addressing the issues.

Without data all you have is an opinion – and your business deserves better.

When bad news is good

Follow up with customers who have stopped doing business with you and find out why. They have not made a complaint or you would know. However, there is usually some form of 'complaint' behind the loss of business unless they have moved from the district or had some other change of circumstance. It is in your interests to find out why someone else is getting the business – Better product? Better service? Better location? Something you did wrong? Something others do better? Make sure you hear what you don't want to hear. This can be an unpleasant conversation for you, but it is one you should have – you need the information to make sure that you are building a great business. Consider this very valuable market research that only costs you a phone call or a visit.

Make customer focus groups work

Getting groups of customers together to discuss your business from their point of view can give you very valuable insights into problems you may be unaware of. Some tips for getting the best from these groups include:

- Make sure that there is a range of views and not just 'pet' clients or customers.

- Don't pay for participation as it will compromise people's honest expression – a small thank you voucher can be a nice touch.

- Let customers talk as freely as possible and don't try to set the agenda.

- Use an external facilitator so that they feel free to speak.

- Be aware that they may wish to flatter you.

- Don't attempt to defend, explain, justify or argue back.

- Have very few of your people at the table as customers will avoid offending.

- Share the results as widely as you can in your organisation.

Feelings matter

When it comes to a transaction, it is customer emotion not logic that is in charge. How they feel at each stage of the transaction is really important. Your staff may need training to deal well with the feelings of complainants. The important things to remember are:

- **Learn to listen** – what is the customer *really* saying?

- **Change perspective** – look at the problem from the client's point of view.

- **Don't take it personally** – the person is upset by the situation, not with you.

- **Empathise** – it's not just the words you use but the feelings you show.

- **Keep quiet** – listen to the end before replying.

- **Address the human side** – make people feel smarter, more confident and secure. We all want that!

And feelings are contagious...

The way your employees feel is the way your customers are going to feel.

You can't have cranky employees and happy customers.
Paul Water, CEO Sears, Canada

FINDING GREAT PEOPLE

If you have the right people in your business it will run itself! If you have the wrong people for your business you will spend all of your time fire-fighting the things that go wrong and trying to 'fix' the people you have. You are hiring your future success or your future problems with every recruitment decision – it's just like picking a football team! And it's your time, energy and money that are on the line. It costs to recruit good people – and it costs even more if you recruit the wrong ones!

Killer Questions

> *Are you building a company of giants or a company of dwarves?*
>
> *Are you hiring in future success or future problems?*

Giants or dwarves?

Every new person you hire either helps to lift the 'average' in the business ... or lowers it. If the new person is 'bigger or better' than most of the existing employees, then your average goes up. Think of it like the bench for a sports team:

- Are you building bench strength with each new person you hire?

- Are you adding the muscle you need to your team?

- Will you end up with a business staffed by the giants of your industry or by the dwarves?

What are you looking for?

It is all too easy to end up filling a vacancy with a 'warm body'. Before you start you need to decide what the job requires. This will help you when you are recruiting, advertising and interviewing. If you are not sure what you need you may well attract the wrong people or hire someone who appealed on meeting with them but who ultimately does not have the right skills for your business. Ask yourself:

- What will this person be responsible for in the business?

- What competencies would this person need to be successful?

- What evidence of prior performance would you expect to see?

- What one major skill/expertise do we need this person to have, e.g. sales/finance (don't try to get them to do everything)?

The table below gives an example of the type of planning that you need to do before you start the recruitment process and that means you will be ready for the interview. A structured approach will prevent you from being 'flannelled' by the candidate.

Key Responsibilities	Competencies	Evidence
Grow Sales	Sales Planning Relationship Development Negotiation skills Closing the deal	Examples of plans Stories of successful relationship development Description of an actual negotiation process Discussion of an actual deal Examples of closing deals Examples of reaching targets

Hire SWANs

The acronym SWAN is a good guide to what you need to look out for when recruiting:

S – Smart: Smart people learn. Where is the evidence of learning? It could be formal, as in qualifications, or through courses they have taken, or there may be evidence of good learning through experience.

W – Works Hard: Valuable employees put their shoulders to the wheel. Look for evidence of making effort in previous jobs and outside of work.

A – Ambitious to Achieve: You don't want to hire someone who intends to 'retire and stay' on full pay in the business! Look for evidence of achievement in previous jobs and in personal life. Setting goals and achieving them is good evidence.

N – Nice: Nice people have good interpersonal skills and their referees will be able to tell you that managers, colleagues and customers liked working with them.

Unless you really need a nuclear physicist or a cardiac surgeon, a SWAN will usually do the trick. Yes, there are specific qualifications required for some roles, but you still need to ask yourself if you are hiring a SWAN. Clearly, you need a *smart*, bright person if they are going to grow and develop with your business. No matter how educated or qualified someone is, you need someone who is in the habit of making an effort and who expects to *work hard*. Your business will be going backwards unless it has people who want to *achieve* something for themselves and for the organisation that they are in. And while you can teach people most things, it takes a lot of effort to make someone who does not like other people *nice*. Try not to hire a terrorist! They alienate colleagues, they assassinate customers and they annihilate your business.

Do you really need a full-time employee?
Employees are very expensive – in direct costs like wages and salaries, but also in indirect ways like management time and effort. You may need the work done but you may not need a full-time employee. The overall costs and

risks may be much lower if you can use an independent contractor, a part-time or casual worker, or an intern. You also get the chance to check people out before you have made all of the commitments.

Attracting a good pool of candidates

It is a big decision to take a job, any job. Good people have lots of choice. Think about how you will present yourself, the business and the role so that it is attractive to a great candidate. Marketing to potential (or existing!) employees is not much different than marketing to customers – the look of your business, the premises, the other staff and the boss. For many small and medium-sized businesses the candidates you will be trying to attract are local, know your business and are known to you or some of your employees. What impression do they already have of your business? Have they already decided that they would love to work with you if the opportunity ever came up?

Advertising

Most job advertisements are extremely boring. Consider doing something different that will stand out:

- asking for help – *We need an amazing person to help us to …'*

- a sign outside the building – *'Talk to us if you would like to join our team.'*

- a picture of the team you want a person to join – make sure they look happy and energised – *'Are you ready to …?'*

- a project you have done or are about to do – *'Would you be interested in …?'*

- an online competition (use your online networks).

Winners work with winners

Wonderful people always know other wonderful people. Ask your existing staff if they know someone who might be suitable. Good staff will be very reluctant to recommend any but the best for their own workplace. Use this technique within your wider network as well – winners always know other winners. Word of mouth is also very effective with good candidates – nothing works as well as recommendations from people you know and trust that this might be the perfect job for you, the candidate.

Use the boomerang

Many wonderful people pass through some businesses. It can be very effective to consider never truly 'losing' a good employee. Sure, many of your people will move on to bigger roles or they may go off on their own. Make sure you never make it very hard for them to go if they want to – that only leads to them hiding their intentions from you. Lay the groundwork to stay in touch – you can continue to invite them to business functions, or you can send them emails to keep in touch while overseas or you can visit them when you are travelling around. The whole idea is to predispose them to return to you (bigger and better than ever!) if that is appropriate and to continue to have such a good relationship with them that they will send other good people your way. They are already expert in what it takes to succeed in your business and who would fit the bill.

Interviewing

It is really easy to get fooled at interviews – we all think we are great judges of character! The better you have done your planning about what is needed on the job, the better you will be able to avoid being fooled by first impressions at an interview. Using the list you drew up about the responsibilities and competencies needed for success, you can devise a checklist of questions to keep you on track. Make notes as you interview – if you have a few people to see it will be very hard to remember later. Interviewing along with another trusted person allows you to listen while another asks some of the questions and also gives you someone to compare notes with afterwards. Your other interviewer(s) could come from inside or outside your business.

The format below is useful for structuring your interview. It means that you will ask all the candidates the same questions and helps prevent the interviewee from 'hijacking' the interview. When you know what competencies you are interviewing for, you can do a page for each of the ones you are seeking. This format allows you to make notes as you go and means you have something to compare at the end.

COMPETENCY: e.g. Management of people		
QUESTIONS	LOOK FOR	NOTES
'Tell us about your management style'	Evidence of standards set, coaching, feedback	
'Describe a difficult employee and how you dealt with the situation'	Awareness, appropriate behaviours, constructive resolution of the issue	
'How do you keep your team motivated?'	Understanding people, a practical approach, warmth towards staff	
'What would your staff tell us about you as a manager?'	Self-awareness, 'firm but fair' type feedback	

Questions to uncover personal qualities:

- What style of management gets the best from you?

- What have you learned from the jobs you have held?

- What have you done that shows initiative in your career?

Questions to address a particular competency, e.g. sales:

- Tell me about the most satisfying/challenging sale you have made recently.

- What attracted you in the first place to a career in sales/marketing/call centre management?

- Describe your typical week as a sales manager in your last role.

Questions to find out interpersonal competencies:

- Tell me about the most difficult person you have ever had to work with and how you handled the difficulties.

- What significant decisions have you had to make recently? What options did you consider and on what basis did you make the decision?

- What do you have to consider if you wish to influence senior management?

Reference checking

Past performance is the best guide to the future. Candidates are often economical with the truth on a CV and many 'problem' people interview very well! Written references are insufficient – nobody ever has a written reference that does not say good things. So you need to talk to previous managers and employers. Thorough reference checking is essential. This takes time and effort, but the expense is minimal compared to making a bad hire. Do remember that people are very reluctant to volunteer information about someone that once worked for them – you will have to ask the right questions, listen for any hint that there is more to be said and probe for the information you need. Most referees won't tell you what you didn't ask – it's not their job to make sure that you hire a good one – it's yours!

- Check the details on the CV – the dates, the roles and the achievements claimed.
- Require verified copies of any qualifications or memberships of associations.
- If using an external agency have a written agreement as to who will be responsible for reference checking.

Make sure you talk directly to previous managers, supervisors or employers – friends, relatives, work colleagues and other community contacts are not objective enough.

Here are some examples of the kind of questions you can ask when checking references to get as much relevant information as possible:

- How would managers describe the candidate?
- How would colleagues describe the candidate?

- How would people who reported to him/her describe the candidate?

- What are the candidate's talents and strengths?

- Which areas does the candidate need to develop?

- Does the candidate lead consistently in a way that inspires others to follow him?

- Do they hold people accountable for their performance and promises?

- Are they comfortable delegating important tasks to others?

- How much time do they spend developing other people?

- Would you rehire this person?

- In what role?

- What reservations would you have?

You will need to ask follow-up questions to many of the above. If there is any hesitancy on the part of the referee, probe gently until you find the issue. Trust your instinct here – and seek more referees until you are satisfied that you have the right picture. This aspect of the selection is the one that is often skimped on – at great cost to your business. Remember, you *must* have the candidate's permission to reference check.

Orientation

Make sure that they get off to a good start. The first few days, weeks and months in a new job leave an indelible impression. Everything should be telling your new hire that they have made a great decision to join you! Don't just throw them in 'at the deep end'. Show them around, introduce them to key customers, appoint a colleague as a mentor if appropriate and check in with them regularly to ensure that they are settling in and getting on well.

LOVE THEM OR LOSE THEM!

Winning in business is increasingly about having – and holding on to – great people. Businesses all around the world know that they can only win if they can find and keep great people. Do you?

There is an international market for people with education, skills, experience and a good attitude – and every business in the world wants them. There is also a worldwide shortage – so much so that McKinsey published a study a few years ago called *The War for Talent*. Can you compete? Predictions are that the worldwide shortage of talent will continue to grow – the wealthier countries are 'vacuuming' up skilled people from other economies, including Ireland. We moan about the 'brain drain', but the trend is likely to accelerate. Although the current economic climate is keeping people in their current jobs in the short term, you should be constantly mindful of what you can do to keep the people you need to make your business thrive.

The answer is: lots. There is a great deal known about what motivates employees and keeps them in your business. We also know a lot about why they leave – the things we need to stop doing!

Killer Question

Would you work for you?

You are the most important factor in people's decision about whether they stay or whether they go. Given that people generally leave because of the way they are managed, have a think about how you relate to your team. Would you love to work for someone like you … or would you simply not put up with your own style of management. Do an audit on what you say, how you say it, what you do and how you do it. You may get a surprise.

Why do they stay?

- Because they are able to do a good job. Great people like to succeed. It's the manager's job to make sure that they can achieve at work so that they can have job satisfaction.

- Because they are learning something. Great people want to develop and grow. Otherwise their job is a dead end and they may even end up unemployable. Make sure they can learn new skills on the job – these might be technical, might be around customers, or be personal development skills.

- Because they are building or creating something. Great people want some meaning in their lives. This doesn't mean they have to be building spaceships, but they do want to know what the business is for, how it helps and where it is going. They love it when you share all of these things with them.

- Because they feel they belong. Great people want to be part of something. If you spend most of every day at work it matters how you feel about the business and the other people in it. Make them all part of the family.

- Because they believe they can be great. Make sure staying in the company will help them achieve this.

The costs of turnover

Even if you really don't care very much about the people for their own sake, have a think about some of the costs of turnover:

- Recruiting costs to find a replacement – either you pay an agency, or use your time and money for ads, travel, etc.

- Time spent interviewing candidates.

- Time in training new people – it always takes more effort and time than you think.

- Cost of the extra time the new person's supervisor or 'buddy' must invest.

- Salary paid to the new person while he learns to do the job.

- Mistakes the new person makes when first on the job.

- Disruption suffered by your business during re-placement.

- All the money you spent finding and getting the previous person up to scratch.

- Lost opportunities and customer dissatisfaction when the job was vacant.

- Loss of knowledge of the business and customers that left with the other person.

You could go on and on. Some of these costs are obvious, e.g. time and money spent finding a new person. Some of them are more hidden, e.g. the loss of knowledge, the lost opportunities, all the money you spent on the departed person. It can add up to a big sum.

Try doing the sums:

Advertising	€300
Agency fees	€2,000 (and could be much higher!)
Your time	€2,500 (two weeks of €60,000 person)
Direct training	€1,000 (time, money, materials, waste)
Getting up to speed	€15,000 (person on €30,000 might take six months?)

Every business will have a different set of costs, especially around disruption, loss of business and of knowledge. Any way you look at it, the sums are sobering.

What do they want?

Believe it or not, it isn't about more money (though you do have to pay 'em!). The Gallup Organisation (the people who started the polls) have surveyed over three million employees and they found that people want quite simple stuff:

- They want **clear expectations** – do they know what you want them to do?

- They want the **resources** they need to do a good job – have they the tools and materials they need?

- They want to **achieve** things – can you provide the opportunity for people to feel that they perform really well?

- They want **recognition** – do you notice what they do, offer praise, or say thanks?

- They want **someone to care** about them – do your people feel that you care about them as well as about the task?

- They want **development** – do you give your people any encouragement to grow and learn?

There was plenty more, but these things are the most important. It isn't hard to provide these things – but it is very easy to overlook them, especially when you are busy and your focus is on other tasks.

Hot tips for keeping them

- Talk with your people as much as possible – about the work, the business, themselves.

- Find out what matters to them and accommodate them as much as you can.

- Make being at work as much fun as possible – you may have someone on your team who is good at this too.

- Get to know them and their families – and listen and behave like you care about them all.

- Be friendly and cheerful – no one wants to work with or for a grump!

- Make the work as challenging or interesting as you can – this is often achieved by talking about what the business is trying to do or discussing the reasons for changes.

- Help people see that they have a good future with you – talk about their progress and the future for the business.

- Ask for their opinions – people like to be included and to share their ideas.

- Do things as a group – go on an outing, have a party, pay for them.

- Say 'thanks' – lots!

- Be as family friendly as you can – people usually care more about their families than work and you should be as flexible as you can.

Appraisal – *for* **you!**

Managers often review or appraise the people who work in their business – they want to assess and rate their performance. But you also need to know what the people think of *you* – how they rate you – as well as how you rate them. If you have enough people to ensure some anonymity you can give them a questionnaire. If it is a small group you may have to ask more roundabout questions like:

- What are some of the things I do that you like and/ or that make me a good employer?

- What are some of the things that I do that you would like me to stop doing?

- Can you suggest things that I could do more of/less of/do differently?

It can be difficult to ask for feedback at first – but people will admire you for making the effort and for being open to hearing their view. If you are truly awful you may want to wait for a while and build up some goodwill and trust first. And it goes without saying that there is no point in asking if you are not going to take any notice of what they say!

Your SWOT as an employer

Even if you are not ready to ask for the opinions of your people about your style of management, you can (in the privacy of your own home or office) do a self analysis of your strengths, weaknesses, opportunities and threats (SWOT) as a manager.

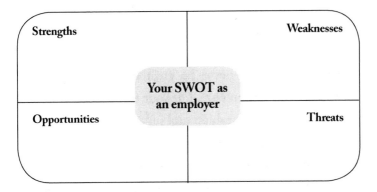

Ask yourself:

- What are the things I am good at as a manager (Strengths)? E.g. I am approachable, I take time to explain things.

- Where am I not so good (Weaknesses)? E.g. I am abrupt and impatient when I am busy, I can be very grumpy when I am worried about sales.

- Where could I improve/get better results (Opportunities)? E.g. a bit of time and money spent on training would get better performance and make people feel more valued.

- What could go badly wrong (Threats)? E.g. if I don't talk to Jenny soon about my expansion plans and her role in that, she may leave for the opposition – I know they'd love to have her.

GETTING THE BEST
FROM YOUR PEOPLE

Your business will never be great unless your people are. It is tempting to put all of your focus on improving your business into products and services, but it is people who make a great business. Anyone can copy your products and services; others will follow your strategies and imitate your marketing. But it is very difficult to replicate a great team of people. Most businesses are quite simple in terms of what they do; it is *how* they do it that makes all the difference. Only your people can give you a competitive edge that is very hard to copy. If you want to be out in front then you should focus on growing great people.

Killer Question

> *What is each of your colleague's understanding of what they need to do to be a success in your business?*
> *What made you great?*

And you are great, aren't you? After all, you set up, or own or run the business – or maybe all three. It didn't happen by accident. Among the many things that helped you become great could be:

- good training
- a great boss
- someone who took an interest in your development
- understanding what needed to be done
- knowing what made the business work
- building up a key strength
- belief in yourself
- others who believed in you
- feeling that what you were doing mattered
- doing things you were good at
- being able to achieve something
- feeling that others valued your contribution.

How many of these are you providing for your people?

What's the job?

To be great people need to know what's expected of them. In many workplaces they only find out when they mess up! It is very difficult to perform well if you are not clear about the expectations. Make sure your people know what you want from them. Be as explicit as possible about the 'what' of the job. In other words, try to describe the end result that you want, e.g. 'Keep the floor clean', rather than 'Sweep the floor three times a day'.

Give them some say in the 'how?'

When possible (and sometimes it is not) it is much more motivating for people if you leave some decisions to them. People feel like cogs in a machine when every step is decided for them and they are treated as if they had no ideas or contribution to make. It would be easy in the above example to require that the floor be swept three times a day each weekday but only once on Saturdays. But maybe it would be better to vacuum it … or maybe to think about ways to prevent it getting so dirty. You will never make people great by taking away all of their opportunities for thinking. People become great by feeling that they have something to offer, by thinking about their work and how it can be done better and by having these contributions valued by their manager.

Help them understand the business

It is impossible for people to be great if they have no idea how the business works. You can help people become interested and knowledgeable about what matters to your business. Things that staff can do to increase their understanding of the business are:

- **visiting customers** (shows what matters to the customer).

- **dealing with complaints** (shows what goes wrong so that it can be fixed at source).

- **looking at the figures** (shows people where you have high costs, or waste, or which products or which customers contribute most).

- **doing some research on customers** (shows what they value; what they dislike).

- **checking out the competition** (shows what the choices in the industry are).

People who understand the business they work in are more interested, more motivated and are able to come up with great ideas about how to increase sales, reduce costs, please customers, do things in better (more efficient, faster) ways.

Train and develop your people

People who are great are always learning. Learning does not have to involve being away from work on expensive training courses – *If you think training is expensive, try ignorance!* Options to consider include:

- showing people how to do the job properly at the start.

- 'buddying' up less experienced staff with others.

- swapping people with another business for a day or a week to see what they can learn in another place (and what you can learn from the visitor).

- helping people set goals for something they want to be better at and supporting them to achieve it.

- rotating people in jobs in your business (even for a short time) so they can see what others do and how the jobs fit together.

- encouraging them to study out of work hours (and refunding/part-refunding them for fees if they are successful).

- setting a group learning goal, e.g. dealing with a complaint, and spending some time together to pool what you know.

- learn at lunch or after work (getting a speaker or having a demonstration or doing a visit – this can be short and sweetened by the provision of some refreshments).

People feel much better about themselves and about their work when they feel that they are learning and improving. Your staff can't be great unless they are getting better all the time.

Give them lots of feedback

Feedback is the breakfast of champions! You can make the people around you great by giving them plenty of feedback about how they are doing. Everybody likes recognition. So make sure that you catch people doing it right and tell them how good they are, how much they are improving, and what a difference they are making to the customer and to the business. It goes without saying that almost all of this feedback needs to be positive – you don't make great people by criticising them! If you are a 'grim germ' you may need to think again about your approach. As a general rule, praise in public. Not everyone likes public recognition but most people do. The bigger your 'winners circle' is, the better your business will be.

Praise in public, criticise in private

As much as possible, give any negative feedback in private. People don't enjoy being corrected in public and it usually achieves little except their resentment. Embarrassing or humiliating your people will work against your business success.

> *Write people's accomplishments in stone and their faults in the sand.*
>
> *Benjamin Franklin*

Moments of Truth

EXERCISE

Try keeping a log of every interaction you have with each of your people for a week. Review your notes:

- Did that contact leave them feeling bigger and better?
- Did it sear their heart and make them feel diminished?
- What is the ratio of happy to unhappy moments?

- Are you making many more deposits than withdrawals in each person's 'trust' account?

- How do you think the person felt about you and your business as a result of the interaction with you?

- How might this be affecting your business performance?

Build on strengths

People will never be great doing stuff they are no good at! You can never be great at your weaknesses. Your job as manager is to find what their talents are and make sure that they get to develop and use that natural strength. If your business has no place for someone's talents or strengths then do yourself and them a favour and help them get a more suitable job. Strengths or talents include:

- organising

- planning

- dealing with people

- doing the core work of your business

- administration

- communicating

- keeping the team happy

- improving systems

- developing new ideas

- getting new clients

- attending to detail
- fixing problems.

Have you got the right people in the right work? Take care of them ... and they'll take care of your business!

Understand their needs

Henry Ford used to complain: 'Why is it that when I want a pair of hands I get a whole person instead?'

It is easy to wish that only the parts of the person that you need come to work – but they actually arrive with a whole life, family, interests, obligations, etc. If you want them to be great in your business you will need to accommodate other aspects of their lives. While it is unwise to get over-involved in the personal lives of your staff, you will want to understand each individual well enough so that you can meet their aspirations, interests and family needs as much as possible. It is in the interests of your business that their personal needs are met – only then are they free to devote their energy to making your business great.

Don't forget to incentivise

Don't forget to incentivise but make sure you incentivise for success. We talk about rewards in the next chapter but it's important in the current economic environment to remember that to get the best from your people there are other valuable incentives that can be used as well as money, e.g. learning and development opportunities; being part of a team of smart people; being shown that you're valued; being encouraged and mentored.

At the end of the day ...

We all go home at the end of each and every day either more motivated and excited about coming back and doing great things tomorrow or less motivated about our work. Making your people great is about the small things that happen every day.

You Get What You Reward

Reward and recognition are amongst the most powerful tools the business manager has. All of us are motivated by the payoff or outcome that we receive. If we feel we are underpaid and undervalued we become de-motivated. At the very least, pay and conditions must be fair compared to others in the industry with similar skill. Better staff will have plenty of choice – it does not pay your business to allow them to feel underpaid or undervalued. Even in times of recession it is important to keep staff motivated by rewarding them when it is possible.

However, it takes a great deal more than adequate pay to make people satisfied and highly motivated to give of their best.

Killer Questions

What is really rewarded in your business?
Is that what you want to reward?
Are the right people the happiest and the best rewarded?

Rewards are more than money

There is plenty of research to show that money is only a

part of what makes up the reward system at work. And once people feel that their pay is fair it is no longer even the most important part. (If they feel that they are being unfairly paid you have a very real problem – show that they are wrong by producing comparisons within your industry and locality or fix the problem by paying appropriately.) Other things seem to really matter to people when they consider how 'rewarding' and motivating your workplace is.

	Rate Your Rewards	Score 1–10
1	Clear expectations about what is expected of them	
2	Challenge and achievement	
3	Promotional opportunities	
4	Career advancement	
5	Good learning opportunities	
6	Participation in decision making	
7	Tools and information necessary to do a good job	
8	Good relationship with immediate manager	
9	Support and respect from management and colleagues	
10	Sense of team and belonging at work	
	Total	

How does your business rate (1–10) on each of the above? What's your score out of a possible 100?

Many of these are 'free' to put in place, but the payoff to your business in attraction and retention may be priceless.

Money is an important component

Contrary to employers' expectations, money never features at the top of people's list of what's important to them at work. However, they are not slaves and you do have to pay them! If they are poorly paid, money will become a source of dissatisfaction and a distraction. The best policy with pay is to pay as well as you can afford – bearing in mind industry rates – and then do everything you can to help people forget about money. Make sure that you keep up with your industry in your location. Expect to pay more for better people with good skills – the returns to your business are likely to be far higher than the monetary cost to you. If you want to outperform other businesses the obvious place to start is with better (and better paid) people. Take money off the agenda as much as possible by paying well and then turning people's attention to what they are achieving, how they are developing and the good lives and secure sustainable business that they are helping create. Whether the economic climate is good or bad the principles remain the same.

Rewarding x and hoping for y

When it comes to basic pay, pay increases, promotions, incentives or bonuses you need to be very sure that you are indeed rewarding what you value. For example, if you hope for teamwork and collaboration, but your system only rewards individual achievements, you can forget about co-operation in your workplace. People will watch what you reward, and money (and other goodies like training or company cars or a nice office) is very measurable. No amount of talk or encouragement will persuade people to change their behaviour (towards colleagues or customers) unless the reward system clearly follows. And if you reward, promote or otherwise reinforce people who flout the values of the business, you create a very unhappy and cynical staff. They simply no longer trust you or believe what you say. You get what you pay for.

What matters to people?

People are motivated to join and commit to a workplace by a number of factors. Base salary or wages is only one, albeit a very important, component of motivation. Other benefits such as pension or health insurance are important. People also value the work experience itself – meaningful work and good people to work with. Personal needs matter too.

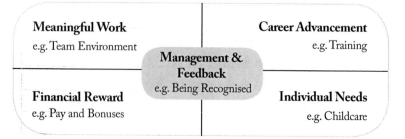

| **Meaningful Work** e.g. Team Environment | **Management & Feedback** e.g. Being Recognised | **Career Advancement** e.g. Training |
| **Financial Reward** e.g. Pay and Bonuses | | **Individual Needs** e.g. Childcare |

The balance between these factors will vary from individual to individual. Each individual may weigh the factors differently from time to time.

Total rewards package

Employees (and prospective employees) will evaluate you on the total rewards package you offer.

How does your business compare with others who are trying to lure your best people away? Are you first or second or third on these aspects?

Aspect of Total Rewards Package	Your Business	Competitor A	Competitor B
Salary/Wages			
Location			
Physical conditions (e.g. offices, parking)			
Amenities (e.g. cafeteria, gym, 'free' products)			
Family friendly (e.g. crèche, childcare allowances, generous leave provisions)			
Flexible hours of work			
Opportunity to work from home at times			
Pension scheme			
Health insurance			
Pay for performance			

Aspect of Total Rewards Package	Your Business	Competitor A	Competitor B
Career opportunities			
Training and development			
Meaningful work (what we do, how we do it)			
Company mission and values			
Management and feedback systems			
Team environment			

If you are seeking to attract and retain people who are better than average, your *total* rewards package will need to be better for the individual in question. You should consider varying the 'package' to suit the individual you are trying to attract or keep, e.g. family friendly criteria may be very important to parents of small children, whereas career opportunities might be more important to graduates. The above aspects can be used as a menu to structure each person's package.

What about incentives?

Incentives are a blunt instrument because they can work so well. The problem is that they may not work quite as you intend. For example, you might incentivise higher sales for the quarter so everyone gets busy selling. But consider how they might attempt to get the increased sales – overstocking the trade (returns next quarter or lower sales next quarter), pressuring customers, under-servicing sales in the interests of just making the top line numbers, selling only the product or service to which the incentive is attached (and neglecting everything else they should be selling and doing), competing with their colleagues rather than collaborating on behalf of the customer and the interests of your (longer term) business, 'booking' next period's sales in this period (you won't notice for a while) and abusing non-sales colleagues who are not included in the incentive programme. Often when an incentive programme is announced the first thing that people do is get busy working on how to 'play' the programme. Incentives encourage people to behave in self-interested ways. Remember: you get what you reward!

If you feel that you want to incentivise your people you need to look out for the sorts of unintended consequences suggested above and make sure that you arrange the incentive in ways that lower the risks to your business. The worst scenario is that you will end up having very highly rewarded poor performers! And if others in your business feel that the system is unfair or that the wrong people are rewarded or that they (e.g. secretaries, support staff) are excluded, you will be likely to do big damage to your business. Handle incentives with great care.

Bonuses
A bonus is usually linked to overall performance for the

year. To work well in the interest of your business the criteria for achieving a bonus must be very clear and should be expressed in numbers, e.g. a level of sales, projects completed on budget and on time to agreed specification, people developed to specified levels of skill, new customers or accounts acquired that meet qualified criteria, etc. The bonus amount will need to be large enough to really be worthwhile, e.g. 10% of base salary or more. The targets to be met must be possible but also need to be a real stretch – otherwise bonuses look like they are a given and are seen as part of the base salary. At this point they provide no incentive at all – it's business as usual.

Ten quick and easy non-cash ways to recognise people

Everyone wants to be appreciated. It is important both to reward the results you want but also to recognise and reinforce the behaviours that you seek in your business.

1. Say 'thank you' in person.
2. Congratulate the person for doing a good job.
3. Write a personal thank you note.
4. Write a letter about the achievement or event and put a copy on the personal file.
5. Provide cake at coffee-break time in honour of the achievement.

6. Stick a thank you post-it on the door or desk (where others will see it).

7. Take the person with you to see a new account or important customer.

8. Praise the person to a visitor to your business, e.g. a client, a director.

9. Have a chocolate award (e.g. a trophy made of chocolate that costs less than €20) for excellent customer service.

10. Send an email to everyone in the business detailing the good thing that happened.

Conclusion

There's a great deal to think about if you are committed to owning a successful business. However, it's important not to overcomplicate things. Business is simple – you need to meet the needs and wants of customers profitably. To do so you must design a business model that can do so. You must also focus on getting the best from yourself and the best from those who work with you. It's simple – but it's not easy! The hard work is to pay attention to these core ideas each day and to keep asking yourself killer questions about your business.

We hope that the ideas we have presented in this book will help you reach your business goals and that you are excited about moving forward and putting some of these ideas into practice. We'd love to hear about your experiences and achievements. We are particularly interested in what you found useful and also the areas in which you'd like further help.

Make sure you get a business – not just a job!

ACKNOWLEDGEMENTS

Much of the material in the chapters 'Three Business Strategies for Success' to 'What's Your Edge?' first appeared in *Live the Dream: Become Rich and Free through Your Business* by Joan Baker (Allen & Unwin, 2006) and is reproduced here with the kind permission of the publisher.

MERCIER PRESS

IRISH PUBLISHER - IRISH STORY

We hope you enjoyed this book.

Since 1944, Mercier Press has published books that have been critically important to Irish life and culture. Books that dealt with subjects that informed readers about Irish scholars, Irish writers, Irish history and Ireland's rich heritage.

We believe in the importance of providing accessible histories and cultural books for all readers and all who are interested in Irish cultural life.

Our website is the best place to find out more information about Mercier, our books, authors, news and the best deals on a wide variety of books. Mercier tracks the best prices for our books online and we seek to offer the best value to our customers, offering free delivery within Ireland.

Sign up on our website or complete and return the form below to receive updates and special offers.

www.mercierpress.ie
www.facebook.com/mercier.press
www.twitter.com/irishpublisher

Name:

Email:

Address:

Mercier Press, Unit 3b, Oak House, Bessboro Rd, Blackrock, Cork, Ireland

Lightning Source UK Ltd.
Milton Keynes UK
UKOW03f2338291013

220025UK00002B/83/P